ONE HUNDRED POTS

Reflections on Sanatana Dharma

Brahmacharini Amrita Chaitanya

Mata Amritanandamayi Center
San Ramon, California, USA

One Hundred Pots
Reflections on Sanatana Dharma
By Brahmacharini Amrita Chaitanya

Published by:
Mata Amritanandamayi Center
P.O. Box 613
San Ramon, CA 94583
United States

In India:
www.amritapuri.org
inform@amritapuri.org

In Europe:
www.amma-europe.org

In US:
www.amma.org

This book is dedicated to Amma—
my love, my Guru, my inspiration

enne aṙiññu ñān ninnil ettum vare
nin taṇalil nī vaḷarttū ammē

O Mother, until I reach you by knowing my Self,
let me grow under your shade.

Contents

Who is Amma?

"If we dive deep enough inside ourselves, we will find that the same thread of universal love ties all beings together. It is love that unites everything."

Amma

Through her extraordinary acts of love and self-sacrifice, Mata Amritanandamayi Devi, or "Amma" (Mother), as she is more commonly known, has endeared herself to millions around the world. Tenderly caressing everyone who comes to her, holding them close to her heart in a loving embrace, Amma shares her boundless love with all—regardless of their beliefs, their social status or why they have come to her. In the past 50 years, Amma has physically hugged more than 40 million people from all parts of the world.

Her tireless spirit of dedication to uplifting others has inspired a vast network of charitable activities, through which people are discovering the deep sense of peace and inner fulfillment that comes from helping others. Amma's teachings are grounded in Sanatana Dharma, the ancient wisdom of India. She teaches that the divine exists in everything in the Universe. Ultimately, realizing this truth is the means to end suffering.

Amma's message is universal. Whenever she is asked about her religion, she replies that her religion is love. She does not ask anyone to believe in God or to change their faith, but only to inquire into their own real nature and to believe in themselves.

Introduction

Whoever we are and wherever we are in the world, we all face challenges. Our lives don't always unfold according to our plans or to our liking. Many factors are beyond our control, sometimes leading to feelings of helplessness, stress, and lack of self-worth. We may experience a sense of isolation, feeling disconnected from the world around us. While most of us yearn for peace of mind and contentment, we may find ourselves grappling with anxiety, anger, or hurt. Moreover, we may react to these situations in a way that worsens our difficulties.

It is here that spirituality comes to our rescue. Over millennia, great masters—such as Mata Amritanadamayi Devi, whom we affectionately call Amma—have guided us to apply the teachings of spirituality in our daily lives. By doing so, we not only find inner fulfillment but also contribute towards building a better world in harmony with nature. We don't need to live in an ashram or have a strict meditation schedule to put these lessons into practice, but rather a sincere willingness to implement changes in our perspective and in how we interact with the world.

The message at the heart of Amma's life and teachings is expressed through *sūrya-bimba-nyāya*—the example of the Sun's reflections:

> *dṛg-ekā sarva-bhūteṣu bhāti dṛśyairanekavat*
> *jala-bhājana-bhedena mayūkha-srag-vibhedavat*

> The Self reflected in all beings is one. It is because of the objects in which it is reflected that it appears as many—like how the one Sun, adorned with a garland

of sunbeams, appears to be many when reflected in various pots of water.[1]

Amma explains, "The Creator and creation are one. If we place 100 pots of water out in the sunlight, we will see a reflection of the Sun in each and every pot. But, in reality, there are not 100 suns; there is only one Sun. Likewise, the consciousness within all of us is the same. Understanding this, just as one hand spontaneously reaches out to soothe the other hand when it is in pain, may we all console and support others as we would our own Self.

Amma's teachings embody the values of Sanatana Dharma, the ancient spiritual wisdom of India. Sanatana means "everlasting," and dharma comes from the Sanskrit root *dhṛ*, which denotes "to hold together" or "to sustain." So, Sanatana Dharma can be understood as "the eternal way to live." As Amma says, "Sanatana Dharma, in reality, is not a religion. It is the sum total of all the principles, pathways of spiritual practice, and customs leading to the spiritual upliftment of everyone."

This book is a compilation of talks I have had the opportunity to give in Malayalam on Sandhya Deepam, a spiritual program on Amrita TV. It is intended to be a practical guide for anyone seeking deeper contentment in their life—anyone seeking to free themselves from a sense of alienation and experience the universal oneness that Amma says is our true nature. This is not just a lofty theory meant to be admired in books but a reality that, with genuine effort, can be experienced here and now. If we reflect on our daily lives, interactions, and relationships, we can gain valuable insights into ourselves and our minds, and begin to develop an inner expansiveness. This in turn, enables

---

[1] Naishkarmya Siddhi 2.47

us to treat our environment and fellow human beings with love and respect, compassion and acceptance.

This book is based on Amma's life and teachings, Indian scriptures, and my own personal experiences. Many of the stories are drawn from two great epics, the Ramayana and the Mahabharata, which are part and parcel of Indian culture. All Indians are familiar with these stories, whether they have heard them from their grandmothers, seen them depicted through various art forms, watched the serialized versions on TV, or read the comic books. They provide a rich illustration of the various facets of human nature.

For those readers who are new to these stories and their characters, summarized versions of each are included at the end of the book.

One Hundred Pots is meant to be a reference book on some of the issues that can arise along our inner journey. You need not read the book in order. You can skip to chapters that interest you, or you can simply open it to a random page each day to find a topic for contemplation.

1

Learning From
the World Around Us

In the Srimad Bhagavatam, Dattatreya shows us that everything in the world has a lesson to impart. During his days of spiritual practice, he took everything around him as his guru. Like Dattatreya, we can also learn to take our own life experiences as opportunities to grow. Every situation we are in, and every person we meet, has a lesson to teach us. Whether we grow in wisdom on life's journey depends on our willingness to perceive, internalize, and put into practice the teachings offered along the way.

Be a Beginner

A few years ago, I was asked to cook for a special guest visiting the ashram. I received a message from the guest's assistant telling me to make puttu (a traditional, steamed dish made of rice flour and coconut) for breakfast the next day. I had never made puttu before. I had only eaten it. So what did I do? I went on YouTube and watched one or two videos demonstrating how to make the dish. They were videos by housewives from their kitchens giving very detailed instructions. The videos clearly showed how to mix the flour and water to get the required consistency, how to fill the puttu cup, add the coconut, and how to steam it.

The next morning, I set to work with confidence. I mixed the water into the flour as I had seen on YouTube. So far so good. It got to what I felt was the right consistency—just as they had said, "It should be like wet sand, holding its shape when pressed in the hand. But also, not too wet." I let it sit for some time. When I put the mixture into the puttu steamer, I felt a little uncertain. It seemed to have become quite dry. But with the confidence I had from my YouTube knowledge, I went ahead, without bothering to show anyone for guidance.

I put the puttu into one of the containers and kept it with the other dishes. The breakfast was collected and taken to the guest. Half an hour later, the person who had delivered the food returned. From his face I could see that something was wrong. He said "Everything else was fine but... the puttu was a disaster! I opened the container in front of the guest, and the puttu just fell apart in front of him. It crumbled into a pile of powder right before his eyes!"

Needless to say, I felt terrible: I had inconvenienced our special guest. And worse still was my embarrassment at having failed in making such a basic and simple dish. Looking back, it is clear to me what went wrong: I had unhesitatingly relied on learning from YouTube. I knew the instructions, and I had all the right ingredients. What I had lacked was the humble attitude of a beginner. I should have realized that, inexperienced as I was, I needed to ask someone for advice. Instead, I was guided by my misplaced feeling that "I know everything," and that attitude led to calamity!

Amma says, "The attitude of a beginner is the doorway to the world of knowledge and expansive vision. It is the attitude of 'I do not know anything. Please tell me.' Humility and an accepting mind come naturally with such an attitude. Grace flows from everywhere, and we become open to gaining knowledge."

On the other hand, if we have the attitude that "I know everything," pride closes our mind down. Our life becomes monotonous and boring; it loses its freshness. Whereas with the attitude of a beginner, we will be able to start every day with enthusiasm, open to all the new experiences and learning we can derive from them.

Although Lord Rama was a complete and perfect being, he took a human birth and set an example for us. Though his knowledge was absolute, he showed us the attitude that we should have towards life—the attitude of a beginner, the humility to ask for advice and the eagerness to learn from whatever situations life brings.

Lord Rama considered the 14 years he spent in exile to be a learning opportunity. Through his many experiences and interactions, he showed us that we can learn from everything and everyone around us. He met many different kinds of people and keenly observed their characters. He learnt from them all. He fondly appreciated the sincere, loyal friendship of Guha and the selflessness of Jatayu. He imbibed the wisdom of exalted sages. He witnessed the dedication and love of Shabari, as well as the organizational skill of Sugriva. He appreciated the mature leadership of Jambavan, the combination of power and innocence in Hanuman, and the integrity of Vibhishana. By closely living with these people, Rama was able to understand and empathize with their needs, interests and concerns. Rama learnt priceless lessons about dharma (right thinking, right action at the right time) not only from great sages and rulers, but also from animals such as monkeys, from a seemingly insignificant squirrel, from the devout and steadfast vulture, and even from demons and others who opposed or criticized him. For a truly wise person, the process of learning is endless.

Amma says "We must always have the attitude of a beginner. An open mind is the hallmark of a beginner. It is humility and the thirst to know and learn. It is the willingness to accept that which is good from any source. If we are able to approach each situation in our life with an open mind, it will awaken patience, awareness and enthusiasm in us. We will be able to imbibe a lesson from any situation. Our life will become a success."

As the Sanskrit saying goes:

yukti yuktiṁ pragṛhṇīyāt bālād api vicakṣaṇaḥ
raver-aviṣayaṁ vastu kiṁ na dīpaḥ prakāśayet

The wise should learn to accept wisdom from anyone, even from a child. Doesn't the small night lamp illumine things the sun cannot?

The receptivity of a beginner will save us from many potential disasters—including in the kitchen!—and enable us to grow into good human beings.

Everyone is Our Teacher

Amma tells us to learn from everything in life. Life's lessons seem particularly abundant in our interactions with others. Moreover, it is usually through them that we best learn about ourselves and how to become better human beings.

Everyone wants to be loved, everyone wants their efforts to be appreciated, everyone wants to be listened to and understood. Whenever someone is kind to us, we can use that experience as an opportunity to grow. If we are able to remember how that incident made us feel, it can become an incentive for us to express similar kindness to others. We can also learn from the bitter experiences. Amma says, "There is a divine message hidden in every experience life brings you—both the positive and the negative experiences."

When I was a student, I had a friend who taught me to be a "good friend." Through her, I learnt things that I hadn't given much importance to before, and how outward expressions of care and appreciation that did not mean a great deal to me were important in building relationships with others. I began to see the value in remembering someone's birthday and marking it in some way, or bringing back a token gift for others whenever I went on a trip somewhere. However small the act may be, such gifts are a mark of appreciation.

Eventually, this friend made some new friends and wasn't interested in spending time with me anymore. She stopped caring: she'd forget my birthday, even though she would be upset if I had been late by a few hours in remembering hers. All her usual tokens of care came to an abrupt halt. At first I felt hurt; I felt she was being so unfair. But after a few days, it occurred to me that I should stop focusing on what a bad friend she was being. Instead, I should think about what kind of a friend *I* wanted to be.

And with that shift in focus, all my feelings of having been wronged vanished. I gained strength and courage. I thought, "Fine, be whatever way you want. I'm not going to get upset over petty things. I will make sure to remain a good friend, no matter what!" She truly had taught me how to be a good friend, through her kindness and care in the beginning, but even more so later, with her indifference and lack of care. Her behavior made it clear to me how I didn't want to be.

This is an attitude lauded in the Mahabharata:

> *yad anyair-vihitaṁ necchad-ātmanaḥ karma pūruṣaḥ*
> *na tat pareṣu kurvīta jānann-apriyam ātmanaḥ*

> What he does not find agreeable when done by others to him, that he should not do to others. He must know that what is unhappy for him cannot be happy for others.[2]

Since then, if someone acts in a way that I feel is hurtful or inconsiderate, I try to learn from that and make a resolve: "May I never cause anyone pain in a similar way." If someone doesn't express their appreciation in a moment that I feel calls for it, I try to reaffirm within, "Let me make sure to be appreciative towards others." When our focus is on our attitude and how true we are to our values, we derive immense strength and courage. It gives us self-confidence because we know that whatever situation comes our way, it will provide us with something to learn from.

---

[2] Mahabharata, Shanti Parva 259.20

To be able to learn like this, we have to remember that we are all interconnected. Just as we have a world of our own, everyone else has a world of their own. Just as we are affected by other people's actions towards us, our actions and words have an impact on others. A harsh word or a turn of the head can really hurt someone. Also, a single smile or gesture of kindness on our part can genuinely brighten up someone's day.

The other day I sent a message to someone I know in Europe to find out how she's doing. It was a tiny gesture for me—just a few minutes of my time. But the next day I got a message back saying, "I can't start telling you how much your message meant to me." Another day, an ashram resident was telling me about the time when her son was in the hospital, 20 years ago or so. To this day, she still remembers the present and caring smile the lady working at the hospital counter gave her. It brought a smile to her face—a smile she carried back to her sick son. Such small actions of kindness require only a little effort, but their effect can go such a long way.

Even though millions of people across the world look up to Amma as their ultimate spiritual guide and inspiration, we often hear Amma saying, "The entire creation is my guru. I have learnt from everything—from trees, flowers, rivers, soil, every single creature, from little children, illiterate people, even from such tiny creatures as ants." If we develop the maturity to learn from all our interactions, we'll grow into good human beings. We will remember how interconnected we are, and stop being stingy with our smile and care.

Welcoming Criticism

The Mahabharata tells the story of two warring groups of cousins—the unrighteous Kauravas and the righteous Pandavas. They both belong to the Kuru lineage and end up fighting for the throne of Hastinapura in a cataclysmic war. The preparations for the Mahabharata War were underway. Bhishma, the commander in chief of the Kaurava army, consulted with Duryodhana about the arrangement of the warriors on the battlefield. Regarding Karna (a great warrior and close friend of Duryodhana), Bhishma said: "O King, Karna always incites you in this war with the Pandavas. He is harsh and boastful. He is not a mighty warrior. He no longer has the divine earrings and armor with which he was born; he has given them away. Parashurama's curse will make him forget his divine weapons when he needs them most. He also has been cursed by a brahmin. Because of all this, in my view, he is only an average warrior." Upon hearing this, Karna exploded in anger. He lashed out at Bhishma, "O grandfather! I am innocent, but you have hated me at every step. You now think I am incapable and a coward. There is no doubt that I think *you* are an average warrior. You have always wished ill to the Kurus and to the entire universe!" He then turned to Duryodhana and said, "O King, what does the dimwitted Bhishma know about the art of war?" He then resolutely declared, "I will not fight as long as Bhishma is alive. I will fight along with the mighty warriors only after he has been slain." Karna couldn't take the criticism of Bhishma. Though Bhishma was very much an elder and had wisdom and insight, instead of responding to his words, Karna retaliated in anger.

We often react similarly when faced with criticism. Amma sometimes laughs about how we react disproportionately at the slightest prick to our ego!

A few months ago, I was sitting at my computer, as I had some work to finish. A notification popped up on my phone. I glanced at it—a friend was asking me for advice. I thought, this is not urgent, I'll reply after I finish my work. A few minutes later, another beep. This time, it was a work-related message, but that could also wait. I continued working. A little later, my mother sent me a photo of the flowers in her garden. Not urgent.

Another message came—this one was from a friend who had watched an online talk I had given. The message expressed her appreciation for it. Not urgent enough to reply now. I stuck to my work. But then came a second message from the same person. I could see only the beginning of the message in the notifications. From those two lines, I understood that she was questioning one of the points I made in the talk. I immediately thought, "What? She's criticizing me? I have to deal with this right now!"

I started thinking of what to send in reply to that criticism— of the justifications I could use to show that I was right and that my friend's criticism was baseless. But right when I was about to reply, it suddenly dawned on me that I was being a fool. I had decided to deal with all the earlier messages I had received later, after finishing my work. What was different about this message? In reality there was no urgency to it at all. The only reason it felt urgent was that my ego had been pricked. At that moment, I realized that my ego couldn't take the slightest hint of criticism.

Amma says, "We do not usually like other people finding fault with us and criticizing us. Many of us become uneasy when we hear criticism. Some become sad, while others react and refute it. Some others even launch a counterattack. Each one of us eagerly justifies our own point of view. But this is not how we should respond to criticism and accusations. If we are willing and alert to accepting them, they can become instrumental in our growth."

Amma often tells the following story: Once, long ago, anonymous articles criticizing the ruler of a country began appearing regularly in a clandestine newspaper. The government hired secret agents to search out the identity of the writer. After a long search, they found him and dragged him before the ruler. The court felt sorry for the poor man, wondering what fate would befall him. But the ruler surprised everyone by saying, "I read your articles. You deeply analyze my actions and intentions. Because of your articles I have understood many issues I had overlooked, and have become aware of my shortcomings. If you become my secretary, I will be able to correct my mistakes and rule the country much better." Amma says that the ruler of the country in this story is an exemplary model for us.

Often, others can see us better than we see ourselves. Amma recommends, "When someone criticizes us, instead of getting angry and immediately reacting, we should contemplate, and we will probably realize that what they said was correct. Because, viewed from outside, the other person is like a witness to our actions. They will see things more clearly. On the other hand, we are identified with our actions. Hence we will miss the mistake we may have committed."

If Karna had been more mature and clear-sighted, he could have reflected on Bhishma's words instead of reacting to them so sharply. He could have avoided the ruthless words he spoke foretelling —almost wishing for—Bhishma's death. And in my case, if I had been a little more mature, I wouldn't have let a small criticism interrupt my focus. Or at least, before jumping into counterattack mode, I could have reflected upon the point my friend was raising. I could have appreciated her honesty and made a little effort to see the situation from her perspective.

Amma says, "The rose is beautiful. But think of the manure that we give to the rose bush. We put cow dung and the dregs of tea leaves. Such manure is needed for bright and healthy flowers to bud and blossom. Similarly, we need the manure of criticism to grow."

Dharma from a Mother

A few years ago, in 2012, a long-distance race was held in Spain. Kenya's champion, Abel Mutai, was in the lead. It was clear to all that Abel was going to win. But Abel stopped running almost 10 meters before the end. He mistakenly thought he had already reached the finish line. The Spanish audience tried calling out to him to go on—but their words were in Spanish, a language he couldn't understand.

By then the next runner had caught up with him. This runner, Ivan Fernandez, could have easily taken advantage of the Kenyan runner's mistake and reached the finish line first. But Fernandez didn't do that. Instead, he gave Abel a push towards the finish line and gestured to him that he needed to keep running. Abel won the race. When asked about what he had done, Fernandez said, "Abel was the rightful winner. He was 20 meters ahead of me when he stopped, thinking he had reached the finishing line. I didn't deserve to win. I did what I had to do."

But actually, in a way, Fernandez did win. He didn't win the race, but his sense of dharma, his honesty, and his integrity won him the respect of thousands across the globe. That moment at the end of the race was captured in a photo that went viral, and Fernandez received a flood of friend requests on Facebook as a result. At the end of the interview, Fernandez said, "If I had just run past him and won, what would my mum have thought of that?"

Amma says, "Mothers are most able to sow the seeds of love, universal kinship and patience in our minds. There is a special bond between a mother and a child. The mother's inner qualities are transmitted to the child even through her breast milk. The mother understands the heart of the child. She pours her love into the child, teaches her child the positive lessons of life and corrects the child's mistakes."

In the Mahabharata, Mother Kunti brought up the five Pandava brothers alone, although only three of them were her own sons; two of them came from Madri, Pandu's second wife. Kunti was a strong, loving mother with noble values, who imparted these values to her sons. Through her own example, Kunti always taught the Pandavas the importance of dharma and of maintaining harmonious relationships with one another.

Another mother might have favored her own sons—Yudhishthira, Bhima and Arjuna—over those of Madri—Nakula and Sahadeva. But Kunti didn't show the slightest partiality towards her own sons. In fact, it was quite the opposite. She gave extra care to Madri's sons, as if to protect them from the pain of having lost their mother.

A fateful dice game took place between Yudhishthira, the eldest of the Pandava brothers, and Shakuni, who played for Duryodhana. Yudhishthira was defeated, and as the price for his defeat, the Pandavas, along with their wife, Draupadi, were exiled to the forest for 12 years. As mother Kunti bade farewell to them, with tear-filled eyes she told Draupadi, "Take care of my sons, Draupadi. I leave my Sahadeva, who is still like a child, in your care. Be not only a wife, but a mother to him."

Kunti passed on a strong sense of dharma to her sons. It was her love and sense of dharma that united them. One day, towards the end of the Pandavas' exile, Yudhishthira found his brothers lying lifeless by the side of a lake. It turned out that it was a yaksha (semi-divine being) who resided in the lake who was responsible. As Yudhisthira came upon his dead brothers, a discussion ensued between Yudhishthira and the yaksha. The yaksha tested Yudhishthira with question after question. Yudhishthira answered them all, passing the yaksha's test with flying colors.

In the end, the yaksha was pleased with Yudhishthira and said, "I grant you a boon. Ask me for the life of any one of your brothers."

Unhesitatingly, Yudhishthira said, "Let my Nakula live."

The yaksha was taken aback. "I am surprised," he said. "I know Bhima is dearest to you among your brothers, and you depend on Arjuna to win the coming war. Yet you choose Nakula's life over theirs—why?"

"O yaksha, my father had two wives, Kunti and Madri. One of Kunti's sons already lives, that is I. It is dharma that one of Madri's sons should also live. So, I chose Nakula."

The yaksha was so pleased with Yudhishthira's adherence to dharma that he granted life to all four brothers. This is just one amongst countless incidents of the Pandava brothers' remarkable faithfulness to dharma. And through all those incidents, it is Kunti's love and high moral values that shine through her sons.

Amma says, "The responsibility of a mother cannot be underestimated. A mother has immense influence over her children. When we see happy, peaceful individuals; children endowed with noble qualities and good dispositions; men who have immense strength when faced with failure and adverse situations; people who possess great measures of understanding, sympathy, love and compassion towards the suffering; and those who give of themselves to others, we will usually find a great mother who has inspired them to become what they are." "Mother" here means any parent or guardian figure who showered love on us during our upbringing.

Amma continues, "The essence of motherhood is not restricted to women who have given birth; it is a principle inherent in both women and men. It is an attitude of the mind: it is love."

The good news is that we all have a "mother" in the divine. This doesn't necessarily mean we conceive of the supreme in a female form. Central to most—if not all—representations of the divine are the qualities of motherhood in their most perfect form: compassion, patience, forgiveness and unconditional love. Although abstract in nature, these qualities become tangible through the bond we have with the guru, the bond we have with a Self-realised soul—whatever the tradition he or she is from, and whether or not they are still in a physical body. Sanatana Dharma describes this bond as the highest form of love. Hence the traditional lines chanted to the guru: *tvam eva mātā ca pitā tvam eva*—"You are both mother and father to me."

Through this bond, the guru showers his or her love on us and in so doing tenderly guides us to become good human beings. The greater the sincerity with which we approach the guru's teaching, the more we will be able to imbibe his or her qualities and grow.

See with Wonder

I have a friend in the ashram who has two children. Though they are two years apart, their birthdays are very close. The son's birthday is the 10th of May and his little sister's birthday is two days before, on the 8th of May. A couple of years ago, I was invited to their room to eat some cake for the little girl's birthday. She was very excited to show me the new dress she had received for her doll. We all sat down and had some of her birthday cake.

Seeing all the attention on his sister, her older brother asked, "Mum, why is it not my birthday yet?" His mother said, "Be patient my darling, your turn will come soon. Your birthday is the day after tomorrow!" The boy was confused. "But Mum, I'm older than my sister, I am two years older than her! So how can it be that her birthday is before mine?" My friend tried to explain to her son, but no matter how much she tried, it didn't make sense in his head. My friend and I smiled knowingly at each other.

Later I thought about the incident, and it occurred to me that this is how we are even after growing up. At that young age, the boy's mind could only understand things to a certain point. He couldn't imagine that there was more to learn, that there was something beyond his understanding.

No matter what the field, our knowledge is always limited. Although there has been huge progress in science, we still have so much to learn even about the human body that is so close to us. What then can be said of our knowledge of the universe beyond that? Our knowledge is restricted. It is laughable how little we know. Although my friend and I felt like laughing at her son's level of understanding, we are in fact not very different from him. We consistently forget how limited our knowledge is and think there is nothing more for us to learn. On the other hand, if we become aware of how limited our understanding is, we will have the humility and openness of a beginner. Only then will we be able to keep learning from everything throughout the course of our life.

The knowledge of a mahatma (great soul) is far beyond our understanding. Amma's knowledge is something we are not able to fathom. Yet at the same time, Amma is a perfect example of humility and receptivity. If we watch Amma's eyes, we can see that for her, everything is always fresh and new. She has the same sense of wonder and innocence that we can see in little children. Nothing is boring for Amma, even though she has done the same thing day in day out for the last 50 or so years. She sees everything as an extraordinary manifestation of the divine. Amma says, "Everything in nature is a wonderful miracle. Isn't a little bird flying through the vast sky a miracle? Isn't a tiny fish swimming in the depths of the ocean a miracle?"

In rare moments, perhaps when beholding the stars on a moonless night, we get a glimpse of what a wonder life is. Scientists say there are many more stars in the cosmos than grains of sand on Earth! Trying to imagine that many of the stars we see are like our sun, possibly the center of a whole galaxy, humbles us and helps us realize how tiny our planet and all the people on it really are. In fact, our so-called great knowledge is laughably narrow. Although a brilliant starry night may inspire awe and wonder in us, it is not enough. We can learn to appreciate that every single thing is a wonder. Often, we rush through our day without pausing to notice things around us. We forget that the very opening of our eyes every morning is a wonder in itself.

Imagine we are stepping out of our house on our way to work. We can take a second to be present in that moment, to take in the world around us. We can feel the warmth of the sun's rays on our skin. The bird that swiftly darts past us, as if oblivious to the busy road's hustle and bustle—let's take time to follow its flight. We can notice the vibrant green of the weed growing out of a crack in the pavement. We can experience the different sensations, sounds, and smells all at the same time... We feel our legs carrying us around without our even thinking about it, without our asking them to do so. We can contemplate the wonder of this.

The list can go on and on. Like this, we can transform the most ordinary moments of our day into moments of amazement. All it takes is a shift in perspective. For that, we need to come to the present moment, stepping aside from the constant chatter of our mind as it ruminates on the past and frets over the future. If we are able to do that, everything will feel fresh, new and unique. We will understand a little more of what Amma keeps telling us—that everything is divine, that this whole world is an amazing manifestation of the divine.

Amma says, "Full of innocence and wonder, the mahatma never gets bored. They are like a child who never tires of hearing the birds sing, who never gets bored looking at flowers, who is always thrilled by the rising moon. Like a child's world, the mahatma's life is filled with wonder. For them, everything is new and everything is fresh."

We may think that Lord Krishna granted his *viśvarūpa-darśana* (the vision of his universal form) to just a fortunate few. But in reality, the world we wake up to every morning is the Lord's *viśva-rūpa-darśana*. We just need the eyes to see it.

After witnessing the Lord's *viśvarūpa-darśana*, Sanjaya says:

tacca saṁsmṛtya saṁsmṛtya rūpam atyadbhutaṁ hareḥ
vismayo me mahān rājan hṛiṣyāmi ca punaḥ punaḥ

Remembering that most astonishing and wonderful cosmic form of the Lord, great is my astonishment, and I am thrilled with joy over and over again.[3]

In the eyes of God, we are like the boy who couldn't understand his sister's birthday; we are unable to understand the essence of the universe. To expand our view, we can try to come to the present moment and look with humility and openness at the world around us.

———

[3] Bhagavad Gita 18.77

2

Be a Warrior

It is on the battlefield that Lord Krishna chooses to impart the teachings of the Bhagavad Gita. This setting is not a coincidence; it is chosen to represent the battle that goes on within every one of us—the battle between our ideals and their obstacles, between who we are and who we can become. This battlefield is within each of our minds. We must become warriors to learn how to fight these internal battles, and truly align our life to the values we believe in.

Heroic Humility

Amma says, "A seed has to bow down to the earth for its real form as a plant to emerge. Only through humility can we grow. Pride and conceit only destroy us. So, live with the firm attitude, 'I am here to serve everyone.' Then the whole universe will bow down to us."

When we hear the word "humility," the first image that comes to mind may be the respect we show to elders, or to images of God or sadgurus, like Amma. But it is not particularly impressive to feel humble when we stand before Amma, or in front of representations of God. Real humility manifests when we are able to bow our heads before every single being because we see the divine in them.

Unfortunately, our world tends to see humility as a sign of weakness, when in reality, it is a sign of great strength. As Amma puts it, "Humility doesn't make you inferior, it raises your dignity, strengthens your character, and helps you attain more clarity of vision and inner expansiveness."

Humility is not some lofty spiritual principle to simply think about and pray for. It is a value that we should try to bring into our daily interactions. Each day is full of golden opportunities to practice humility. The challenge is that we are identified with our ego. Most of the time we think we are right and are unwilling to try to look at a situation from someone else's perspective. We are seldom willing to make compromises. Because almost all of us are like this, to differing degrees, sparks can fly in our daily interactions!

A few months ago, a student came to confide in me. He was feeling unsettled because he found himself locked in a confrontational situation with another person. What had started as a friendly discussion ended up as an argument. To make matters worse, he had walked away abruptly, in a way that may have come across as rude and disrespectful. He felt uneasy about the incident and was still annoyed about what the other person had said. I told him not to worry and tried to distract him with a funny story.

The next morning, when I saw the student, I immediately noticed the relieved expression on his face, as if a weight had been lifted. He told me he had just gone to the person he had argued with and apologized. He hadn't changed his mind about his view of the issue, but he realized that it takes two to have an argument and that he was partly to blame. He apologized for having acted in a disrespectful way. The other person had not expected an apology at all and was completely taken aback. After a few moments she apologized too and admitted that she had gotten a little carried away herself. The two of them then went on to share a respectful conversation about the exact same matter they had disagreed so vigorously about the day before.

Reflecting on this incident, it struck me how noble it is to be able to say, "I'm sorry." We may think it's a sign of weakness, but in reality it's a tremendous sign of courage. What holds us back from saying "sorry"? It is our ego, our insecurity, our fear of appearing vulnerable and exposing our weaknesses. We shouldn't be too hard on ourselves; we all have inadequacies. We all encounter situations in which we say things in the heat of the moment that we don't really mean. Being able to recognise when we do this and admit it to others is a sign of honesty and courage. When we are unwilling to acknowledge our shortcomings, our relationships can reach a deadlock—each person standing on the fortress of their ego, waiting for the other person to give in.

In the Ramayana, there is a wonderful story of a noble warrior who apologizes. He is a character we are all very fond of, Lakshmana.

Having helped Sugriva, the vanara[4] king, regain his lost kingdom, Rama and Lakshmana were waiting in a mountain cave outside Kishkindha[5] for the rainy season to pass. Only then could they search for Sita. The monsoon rains subsided, but there was no sign of Sugriva and his vanara army. By this point, Rama's grief at his separation from Sita was unbearable. At his request, Lakshmana set off towards Kishkindha to remind Sugriva of his promise to help Lord Rama. Distressed at his beloved brother's agony, Lakshmana worked himself into such a rage that the vanaras guarding the gates became terrified upon seeing him approach. He stormed into the palace and confronted Sugriva. He spoke to Sugriva fiercely, accusing him of lying when he had sworn to help Rama find Sita.

It turned out that Lakshmana's anger was a little out of place because Sugriva had already started making preparations for the search. Realizing this, Lakshmana calmed down. He praised Sugriva, and then said: "Sugriva, with your support, Rama will surely vanquish our enemy. For my part, I spoke so harshly to you because I have been with Rama during these four months of unhappiness and have heard his grief-stricken words. I cannot bear seeing him suffer like this. Please forgive me for the words I spoke impulsively."

The great Lakshmana actually apologized. It takes true magnanimity for one person to apologize to another. We see

---

[4] Monkey
[5] This happens during Lord Rama's exile in the forest: Sita has been kidnapped by Ravana, the demon king. When Rama and Lakshmana met and befriended Sugriva, the latter promised to assist them in finding Sita.

here in Lakshmana a true expression of virtue. In this world no one is beyond error, and consequently no one is beyond acknowledging their mistakes or shortcomings. In fact, both Sugriva and Sita at different points in the Ramayana declare: *na kaścid na aparādhyati* ("No one is flawless.")

Amma says, "In a cyclone, large trees and buildings are uprooted, but no matter how strong the cyclone is, it cannot harm the grass. That is the greatness of humility." Real heroism and bravery manifest when we are able to acknowledge our limitations, when we are truthful both with ourselves and with others. Having clarity about our own shortcomings makes it much easier for us to be patient and understanding with others. If on the other hand we are intent on projecting a flawless image of ourselves, we will always harbor fear and insecurity.

We tend to forget that humility brings joy. It is actually an excellent self-experiment—try it out and see how it affects our attitudes and our day. When we feel humble, we feel grateful. It's not possible to feel grateful and depressed at the same time. When we feel grateful, we naturally feel content and our outlook on the world becomes more optimistic.

Virtue Here and Now

There is a famous Malayalam song about king Mahabali's reign that is often sung during the Onam festival:

ādhikaḷ vyādhikaḷ onnumilla
bāla-maraṇaṅgaḷ kēḷkkānilla
kaḷḷavumilla catiyumilla
eḷḷōḷamilla poḷivacanam
kaḷḷappaṙayum ceṙu nāzhiyum
kaḷḷattaraṅgaḷ maṫṫonnumilla

When Mahabali, our king, ruled the land, there was neither anxiety nor sickness. Deaths of children were unheard of. There were no lies, there was neither theft nor deceit, and no one was false in speech. Measures and weights were right, no one cheated or wronged their neighbor.

Mahabali was a truthful, dharmic leader who loved and respected all his subjects. Under his rule, people enjoyed equal distribution of wealth, good healthcare and a society free of corruption.

We might say, "That's all very well. This is painting a beautiful picture, but how does it apply to us? What influence do we have on the state of society? This is a message that has to go to leaders—not to ordinary people like us!"

But in reality, each one of us is the leader of *something*. We may not be the leaders of a country or of a big institution, but we are leaders at our workplace, amongst our friends or in our homes. First and foremost, each one of us is the leader of our own life, and our actions have an impact on those around us. The example of Mahabali's leadership stands to inspire us all to lead virtuous lives, for the benefit of every member of society.

Amma says, "Every action we perform—consciously or unconsciously, alone or as a group—reflects in every corner of the universe. Things won't work if we wait for others to change. Even if they do not change, we should be willing to change. Our focus should be on what we can do."

Efforts towards building a just, honest and kind society, like that of Mahabali, need to start at the individual level. Each of us can strive to embody Mahabali's noble qualities, values such as truthfulness, integrity and kindness, in our day-to-day lives. We may think we are doing that already, but if we scrutinize our thoughts and actions, we will probably find we still have quite some progress to make.

For example, I consider myself to be very truthful, but I still remember clearly how I surprised myself a few years ago. I had made a careless mistake, but it hadn't come to my notice. Someone pointed out my error. They asked, "Someone told me you made a mistake. Is it true that you did such-and-such?" I knew I was to blame for it, but without pausing to think for a moment, I said, "Oh no, that wasn't me. They are mistaken, it must have been someone else."

I walked away from that interaction and immediately felt shocked at my own behavior. The shock quickly grew into guilt. Right away I sent a message to the person, apologizing and admitting that the blunder had indeed been mine.

My behavior in this incident reveals something about the nature of the mind: There is a gap between the values we hold and our ability to remain true to them in practice. If I had taken the time to think and plan my response, I would probably have been truthful. But in the spur of the moment, my spontaneous reaction was to lie. For what? To save my image, to avoid getting into trouble and to avoid embarrassment.

It is because of the imperfections in human nature, such as our tendency to be deceitful, arrogant, impulsive and so on, that there is a need for spiritual instruction in the first place. If it was inherent in us to be truthful, there would be no need for the Upanishads to say, *satyaṁ vada*—speak the truth. If we were naturally kind to our fellow beings and concerned about their welfare, there would be no need for the scriptures to say, *dharmaṁ cara*—follow dharma.

Instead of looking around and complaining about the erosion of values in society, we can look within and see how *we* can better manifest those principles in our own thoughts, words and actions.

Amma says, "Instead of pointing our finger at others, we should try to look at our own weaknesses. If we can make our own mind clear and bright, the world will soon follow suit. Let us light the lamp of new life, the light of goodness, the light of knowledge that dispels the darkness of ignorance. We may wonder, 'How can this dense darkness be removed if I light this tiny lamp?' If each one of us lights a small lamp, the strength of the light will multiply, and everything can be illuminated."

Amma gives us practical instructions on how to do this: "Every night we should contemplate, 'What good did I do today? Did I hurt anyone? Did I get angry with anyone? How can I prevent myself from making the same mistake tomorrow?' If we have spent some time helping others, we should think, 'How can I do more tomorrow? How can I speak even kinder words tomorrow?'"

Remembering the glory of society under Mahabali's rule, we can try to make our own lives shining examples of honesty, kindness, straightforwardness and fairness.

Gratitude:
a Gateway to the Divine

We hear from spiritual teachers, mahatmas and our scriptures that God is all-pervading. Amma tells us over and over that we are surrounded by the divine all the time, and yet we are unable to experience this. In fact, we sometimes feel that the sacred is very distant and far-removed from our daily life. In a way we are like a fish complaining of thirst, while swimming around in a freshwater river.

While at university, I was speaking with my friend who worked at the administration office. During our conversation, she was asked to deliver an urgent message to a student. It was 10:00 at night but apparently the message couldn't wait till the next day. I offered to go along with her to keep her company. When we reached the corridor where the student stayed, we were happy to see her light was on. My friend knocked on her door and said, "Excuse me, sorry to disturb you."

"What is it?" came the reply. It was an exchange student from Spain.

"I've come from the university office, and I have an urgent message for you. Please open the door."

No response.

Thinking there might be a language issue, my friend tried to say the same thing in the little Spanish she knew.

The voice from behind the closed door said, "It's inconvenient for me right now; it is 10 pm!"

"Please, I'm from the office, and it's urgent."

The student said, "No, no, no. Isn't this past office hours? I'm just about to go to bed, and I'm in my pajamas. If there actually is a message for me at the office, I can pick it up tomorrow morning."

My friend started feeling a little exasperated: "Please cooperate. I promise the office has sent me. And you don't need to change your clothes, pajamas are fine—just please open the door!"

By then, some students in neighboring rooms had heard the commotion and had come to see what was happening. They were all amused to eavesdrop on this unusual conversation through a closed door. Finally, the Spanish student decided to open the door. The second she saw my friend with her university ID badge, she gasped, "I'm sorry, I'm so sorry... I thought it was some students playing a prank on me!"

In the end, we all saw the funny side of the event and enjoyed a good laugh together.

Thinking back on the incident, it occurred to me that this is what happens in our lives when we repeatedly fail to recognize God's call. The divine is all around us, constantly—in every person we meet, in every situation we experience. God is knocking at the door of our heart every moment. Unfortunately, we're unable to hear the call, or we misunderstand it. We tend to keep the door of our heart tightly closed. We have built the fortress of our ego, and feel safe, confined within its narrow walls. Our feeling of comfort in the darkness of our self-centeredness stops us from opening the door and letting the light of the divine enter.

This explains why we are unable to experience God, who is the very substance of this creation: *sarvam āvṛitya tiṣṭhati* ("He pervades everything in the universe.")[6] Amma says, "We are

---

[6] Bhagavad Gita 13.14

completely surrounded by God. Everything we experience in life is actually God. The world is nothing but God's clothing." How can we make this part of our experience? How can we open the door of our heart to God's light?

There is one very simple trick to help us open our heart and become attuned to the divine: developing an attitude of gratitude. Amma repeatedly says, "A feeling of gratitude towards everything, towards everyone—this is the attitude we should try to cultivate."

It's not always easy to embrace this attitude in today's society. Gratitude means appreciating what we have right now, whereas social media updates keep bringing our attention to the gap between what we have and what we "should" aspire to have. This may come in the form of the model of car we drive, the outings and holidays we go on, the brand of clothes we wear and so on. Advertisements are constantly trying to convince us that we are missing out if we don't acquire such-and-such a product.

Often, we only realize how much we appreciated something when it is taken away. Imagine we wake up one morning with some ache or pain. It'll bother us and all day we'll be thinking, "If only this pain was gone, if only this one problem was solved, everything would be alright." And when the pain finally goes, we feel so grateful. Sadly, this gratitude is usually short-lived. It may last a few hours, a day—at most two—and then it fades away. Almost inevitably, we fall back to our default position of taking things for granted. In reality, we have so many things to feel grateful for. It may be a healthy enough body, a helpful coworker, a roof over our head, a trusted friend or the song of a bird chirping outside our window.

The special thing about gratitude is that it's impossible to feel grateful and depressed at the same time. When we feel grateful, our whole outlook becomes positive. The more gratitude we feel, the less room there is for negative thoughts.

When our negative thoughts and emotions dissipate, we become open and receptive. We become able to notice little signs of the presence of the divine in our life. We are able to hear the knock at the door of our heart.

> *śūram kṛtajñam dṛdha-sauhṛdam ca lakṣmīḥ*
> *svayam yāti nivāsahetoḥ*

The Goddess Lakshmi[7] comes of her own accord to reside with one who is brave, has consistent gratitude and a gentle heart.

---

[7] A form of the divine Mother, Goddess of fortune

The Motherhood Within:
a Magic Tool

The Upanishads, India's gift to humankind, contain powerful statements (*mahāvākyas*) that reveal the highest goal of life: *Prajñānaṁ brahma*—"Consciousness is brahman (divine)"; *ayam ātmā brahma*—"This atma (Self) is brahman (divine)"; *tat tvam asi*—"You are that"; *ahaṁ brahmāsmi*—"I am brahman (divine)".

To put these teachings in Amma's simple words, "The creation and the Creator are not two. The same Self that is in me is in you, and in all beings in the universe. To realize this truth is the ultimate goal of life." In the bhajan "Ōmkāra Divya Pōruḷe," Amma sings:

> *ennile ñān āṇu nīyum... pinne*
> *ninnile nīyāṇu ñānum*
> *kaṇṇu kāṇāykayāl bhinnamāy tōnnunnu*
> *bhinnam allennāl-itōnnum*
>
> You are the "I" in me and I am the "you" in you. The blindness of ignorance creates the feeling of difference; in truth, nothing is separate.

Every moment of Amma's life is a reminder of this goal. However, in our current state, it might seem a bit of a leap. How can we suddenly switch to recognizing others as ourselves? Most of us are living in ignorance, in a state where we believe that our worlds revolve around "me" and "mine." From this starting point, how can we reach that expansive vision, where all is considered our own Self?

This is where Amma offers us a first-class tool. It is a magic tool to help us expand our vision and break down the narrow walls we have built up around us. That powerful tool is motherhood. Amma says that "universal motherhood" is a treasure within each of us, men and women alike. She is referring to qualities such as love, compassion and patience that are dormant within.

Amma once mentioned this during an evening bhajan session. She explained that during bhajans when we sing about and pray for the "victory" of the Divine Mother, it is a prayer for motherhood to be victorious—for the love and patience within to conquer selfishness and intolerance. Amma said that when we develop that sense of motherhood, spontaneously we will be able to forgive others and forget their shortcomings and mistakes.

We all have some people that irritate us a little at times, for various reasons. It may be due to our judgements about their personality, or based on their actions or demeanor, or it may be because of some bitter experience we have had with them in the past. This can happen anywhere—at home, at work, within our social circle or among relatives. Amma says, "Just as we feel love towards some people, we also dislike some others, for no specific reason."

A few years ago, there was someone I was not particularly fond of. I used to feel irritated with her, and on top of that, I used to feel irritated towards myself for feeling irritated! I wanted to follow the ideal that Amma presents before us of being loving towards all. But however much I tried, I simply couldn't make myself feel love for this particular person.

Then, one day, she was diagnosed with a minor health problem, and the doctor instructed her to eat ragi kanji (black millet porridge). Those days I worked in the kitchen, so I was asked to make the ragi kanji for her evening meal. Every day I would make it and keep it in a closed dish for her to collect.

After a few days I noticed that a change had come about within me. Effortlessly, I was starting to feel love towards that person. Nothing had changed in her attitude or character, or even her behavior towards me. So, what had changed? It dawned on me that cooking for this person had awoken a motherly attitude in me. The action tapped into an internal feeling of motherhood, so I naturally started feeling loving and patient towards her.

I was very relieved. It's much more pleasant to feel open and patient towards someone, than negative and judgmental. This incident was a real eye-opener. It reminded me of the speech Amma gave at an international conference in Geneva in 2002. "Anyone—woman or man—who has the courage to overcome the limitations of the mind can attain the state of universal motherhood," Amma said. "The love of awakened motherhood is a love and compassion felt not only towards one's own children, but towards all people, animals and plants, rocks and rivers—a love extended to all of nature, all beings."

Amma is the ultimate example of the state of universal motherhood, right here before our eyes. When presenting Amma with the Gandhi-King Award in 2002, the renowned primatologist and anthropologist Dr. Jane Goodall said, "Amma is God's love in a human body." Indeed, Amma is a torrent of love flowing across the world and breaking all boundaries. The fact that Amma embodies all of the qualities of a mother figure carries an important message for humanity: in this age of individualism, selfishness and intolerance, the all-forgiving, all-embracing love of a mother is the way forward.

Amma's goal is to relieve our sorrows and make us happy, but also to inspire us to become instruments of love. When we feel motherhood within, we are the first to benefit. Only when our heart is flooded with the light of love do we realize how selfishness darkens our outlook. Trying to develop love towards all beings is a sure way towards our own happiness.

If we put this into practice, we'll find it works like a magic trick. When we notice a negative thought about someone arising within, we can try to imagine that person as our child or close relative. We can try this on our colleague or our neighbor, and speak a few kind words along with a smile. We can try to see them as our own. Such an attitude wipes our mind clean of negativities in an instant. As we keep trying to wipe it clean through such *bhāvana*, or imagination, the character of our mind will gradually become a fit recipient for light and contentment.

> *mātā yathā svīyaṁ putram*
> *āyuṣā ekaputram anurakṣati*
> *evam api sarvabhūteṣu*
> *mānasaṁ bhāvayet aparimitam*

Just as a mother, at the risk of her own life, loves and protects her child, her only child, so too one should cultivate this boundless love to all that live in the whole universe.

———

3

Be a Friend to Yourself

In the Bhagavad Gita, Lord Krishna tells us that we ourselves are our own best friend and our own worst enemy. We ourselves are the only companion that will be with us throughout this lifetime. Just as we take care with the type of friends with which we surround ourselves, we should also pay attention to the kind of friend we are to ourselves. Amma tells us that if we become a good friend to ourselves, our path will be strewn with flowers.

Begging for Love

Amma says, "Even though people exchange beautiful and flowery words about love, somewhere deep down inside, most people believe love is really about taking. In reality, love is about giving. Only through giving love can we grow and help others to grow. If this giving attitude is absent, then the so-called 'love' will cause suffering for both. We shouldn't think, 'Are they a good friend to me?' Rather we should think, 'Am I being a good friend to others?'"

Once, I was asked to give an important talk. I felt nervous as I didn't know if I'd be up to what was being asked. Hoping for some advice and moral support, I decided to talk it over with a friend. I was just about to call her when I realized that she might be busy, so I sent her a message, "Can I call you now?" After half an hour, there was still no reply, so I sent a second message, "It's not super urgent, but when you have time, could you call me?"

I went on with my day. Every time the phone rang, I would hope it would be her. By the end of the day, I felt a little dejected and thought, "It's obvious she doesn't care. Even if she has had a busy day, she could have found a few seconds to message me that she couldn't call. She must have read my messages and simply forgotten about them."

In the evening, I saw her from a distance, and we waved. A few minutes later, a notification popped up on my phone saying, "I saw your messages, I'm sorry, I had a busy day..."

My mind started ranting again: "This is the first time I've ever asked her to call like that. It's clearly something that matters to me. She just didn't care enough to remember."

A battle started raging in my mind. Amma often says that spiritual life is like a battlefield—a battlefield in the mind. On one side was the part of me that wants spiritual progress, that wants to become a better human being. It was saying, "Come on, have some maturity. See this as a test for you. If you depend on others like you did today, suffering is guaranteed. Why does the love and care of others matter so much to you? Shame on you! You are supposed to be a spiritual aspirant. That's your main job in life! Why are you allowing such a trivial situation to affect you?"

On the other side was the part of me that is like a petulant child: "No, it's not fair! I don't want to just let this go. I am always present for *her* when *she* needs it. She has to realize what a bad friend she is!"

As this inner battle waged on, I felt disheartened. I knew what the right attitude was, yet was unable to put it into practice and stop my negative thinking. I tried reminding myself of various spiritual teachings but nothing was working. The hurt feeling wasn't going away. It was then that a passage from the Ramayana that I had read that morning, came to my mind.

In this scene, Lord Rama had helped Sugriva regain his kingdom, and Sugriva was enjoying life to the hilt as the king of Kishkindha. Meanwhile, Rama and Lakshmana were living in the nearby mountains, waiting for the monsoon season to pass. Only then could the search for Sita begin.

These were four very long months for Lord Rama. Every moment he was consumed by the fire of separation from his beloved Sita. At night, he would lie down but couldn't sleep. He was absorbed in thoughts of Sita, wondering about her whereabouts and worried about her safety. As the days dragged on, Rama felt there would be no end to his misery.

Meanwhile, in Kishkindha, Sugriva was living a life of self-indulgence. He immersed himself in sensual pleasures, surrounded by music and dance. He had forgotten all about Rama's suffering and the promise he had made to help him. Finally, after a fierce threat from Lakshmana, Sugriva came to see Rama.

As soon as he arrived before Rama, Sugriva prostrated on the ground, his head touching Rama's feet. He begged forgiveness for the delay he had caused in starting the mission. Rama lovingly raised him up and embraced him. As Sugriva rested his head on Rama's chest, in that moment, he realized Rama's love was the most precious gift he could ever receive.

This is the scene that came to my mind—Rama embracing Sugriva with such love. Rama doesn't hold any resentment against him. There is absolutely no sense of, "You forgot about me. You don't care about me, even after all I have done for you. While I was sinking in an ocean of sorrow, you were simply enjoying yourself." No. Rama has only love—unconditional love.

What nobility of character! A wave of inspiration swept over me. With that image of Lord Rama, Amma's words came to my mind: "Don't be a beggar for love. Strive instead to be a giver of love." It dawned on me that in my insistence that my friend should care, I was actually begging for love. That is the last kind of person I want to be. It is much more rewarding to strive to become a giver of love—a generous giver of love.

I realized that my negativity had made me jump to conclusions without knowing my friend's side of the story. I had forgotten all the times that she had given me her loving support. I began to feel grateful for this incident, as it had shown me my selfishness and inspired me to grow out of it. I had received a precious lesson.

Amma says, "Love is the only wealth that makes a person more happy to give than to receive. It is the wealth we possess but do not see. So, let us awaken the love that we have inside. Let it be expressed to the world through all our actions, words and gestures. Let us not limit love within the walls of religion, faith or caste. Let us allow it to flow freely everywhere. May our hearts embrace one another and awaken and share the blissful love inside us. May love embrace all beings and flow. Then our lives will become blessed."

Keep Control of the Remote

Once, I was preparing for a talk in Malayalam. It takes me a lot of time and effort, as this is not my native language. For some reason, it works best for me to pace back and forth while I practice. I usually like to go to the terrace of a building that's reasonably quiet to walk and recite my text out loud. I may look a little funny to others as I walk up and down talking to myself, but actually, I'm practicing my Malayalam.

That particular morning as I paced, there was a young devotee, a visitor from another country, doing yoga on the terrace. At some point, the sun became too bright where I was, so I moved to the side that was still in the shade. I ended up being quite close to the young yogini. After about 10 minutes, I heard an, "Excuse me!" I turned around and saw it was her. She continued, "Would you mind walking on the other side?"

My Malayalam monologue must have been bothering her. I immediately felt irritated and said, "No, it's too hot on that side. It's fine... I'll just go." I grumpily headed back towards my room, as the young woman happily continued her yoga, unperturbed. I, on the other hand, was left feeling very irritated. Immediately thoughts started running through my head: "Where's the respect? She is younger than me and also just a visitor here. Who is she to ask me to go elsewhere? And anyway, I was speaking so softly."

In that moment, I caught myself. I observed my stream of thoughts and realized I had two options before me: I could go on and on complaining in my head and exacerbate my annoyance.

Or I could take this situation as an opportunity to practice equanimity and continue my day with a positive mindset.

I chose the second option. Not only did I regain my mental composure, I also had a good laugh seeing how little it had taken for my peace of mind to be disturbed. Just as importantly, I realized that I now had a perfect little anecdote to illustrate one of the great principles of spiritual life: *samatvam* (equanimity, evenness of mind).

This is a principle Krishna talks about repeatedly in the Bhagavad Gita. For instance, in the second chapter, when talking about the characteristics of a *jñānī* (wise person), he says:

> *yaḥ sarvatrānabhisnehaḥ tat tat prāpya śubhāśubham*
> *nābhinandati na dveṣṭi*
>
> The *jñānī* remains unattached under all conditions and is neither delighted by good fortune nor dejected by tribulation.[8]

The *jñānī* remains stable, no matter what challenges come his way. He doesn't soar to the sky in times of success. Nor does he sink to the depths in times of failure.

In the Gita, whenever Krishna talks about the qualities of a *sthita-prajña* (one of steady wisdom), it is not for the benefit of the *jñānīs* or for those already endowed with knowledge of the Self. Rather, Lord Krishna explains these qualities for the sake of *ajñānīs* (ignorant people) like us. We are to consider the characteristics of the *jñānī* as *sādhanas* (spiritual practices). They are ideals, for us to practice and strive to attain.

It is clear that for someone engaged in spiritual practices such as meditation, equanimity of mind is needed to be able to focus.

---

[8] Bhagavad Gita 2.57

But if we think for a minute, we will realize that this capacity to remain unperturbed by external situations is invaluable in all fields of activity.

For instance, the success of the student depends on their ability to apply themselves and concentrate, as a mind troubled by external situations will have difficulty focusing. The same applies to someone who, for example, is learning a new job or learning to play an instrument. If we have evenness of mind, focus will come naturally, and we will be more efficient in everything we do. We will also be more present in our interactions with others.

Amma gives us a very simple image to explain *samatvam*: "Letting people and external situations disturb your mental peace is like giving them the remote control of your mind." The primary tool at our disposal to improve evenness of mind is developing the mental strength to keep that remote control in our own hands. Unfortunately, we rarely use this tool, choosing to let people and situations determine our mood and mental well-being instead.

Imagine you were not reading this but instead were watching me say it on TV. The remote control is in your hands. If you are bored by what I am saying, you can easily press the button and change the channel. In such a situation, would you want to give the remote to someone else and let them decide what you watch? No way. Yet that is what we do with the remote of our mind. Whenever we get angry, upset or irritated by someone's words or actions, we are handing them the remote.

In my little incident on the terrace, if I had continued feeling angry and disrespected by the young woman, it would have been like handing over the remote control of my mind to her.

Like this, equanimity is a secret to our mental well-being and success in many areas. How are we to develop it? Amma gives us a simple tool, a little trick to help us with this. She says, try and create a little time gap between your thoughts and your actions. When we don't do that, our thoughts may be expressed as emotional outbursts. If we can create just a little gap, we will gain more control over our emotions. That precious gap gives us a chance to become aware of how we are reacting. We can keep hold of the remote and choose the channel we prefer.

Change the Attitude, not the Situation

Amma says "Happiness is not located in material objects. Had it been, why is it that the same objects fail to give happiness to everyone? For instance, when one person smokes, you will see another person move away from that spot holding their nose. In reality, our experience of happiness depends upon our mind. When the mind becomes peaceful, we will experience happiness without any problem."

Several years ago, the place where I worked had a gate at the entrance. Many of the people working there would grumble about it. This was because every time we'd come in or out—and that would be many times in the day—we'd have to unlock the gate and then lock it up behind us. One person in particular was very reluctant to cooperate with the "locking the gate" rule. He complained about it the most.

After a few months, one of the gate's hinges broke, so it took a lot more effort to open and close. The gate would scrape against the ground, making a loud noise. We'd have to lift its weight when opening and closing it. It was now a two-handed job. If you were holding something, you'd have to find a place to put the bag down. You would have to open the gate, turn around, pick up your bag and put it inside. You'd then have to come back to close the gate. Now, everyone was complaining! The worst was when it rained. We'd have to go through all these steps while somehow trying to hold an umbrella over our head. Fortunately, after a few weeks, the gate was repaired. Suddenly, the gate felt so easy. It felt effortless and smooth, and was a joy to open and close. Even the person who used to complain the most said, "This feels as easy as pressing a button on an automatic door!"

What happened here? The exact same gate that we had complained about earlier had become a source of joy and relief a few weeks later. There was no change in the actual object: the gate was exactly the same before it broke as it was after getting repaired. This gives us an important message: The most important factor isn't the external situation itself, but our attitude towards it. Our happiness depends greatly on how we respond to situations that come our way.

What determines how we respond to a situation? The mind. The mind makes a good servant, but not a good master. However, with training, we can become the master and let the mind be our obedient servant. We can learn how to use the mind and not let the mind use us.

Usually, when we purchase a machine, it comes with an operating manual. But here, we have the subtlest of machines within, and we have no idea how to use it properly. Instead of operating the machine with skill, we let it operate us. Schools and universities remain silent on the subject. They teach us nothing about the art of managing the mind.

Amma says there are two kinds of education: education for life and education for livelihood. Spirituality is education for life. It provides us with the instruction manual to our own mind. It gives us the theory and the practical training to use our mind in a productive way. Thus, through spirituality, we can tame and train our mind, transforming it into a beneficial tool.

The difference between the Pandavas and Kauravas was not in skill, nor strength, nor intelligence. Rather, it was their attitude towards life and people. The Mahabharata War was a war of attitudes. Duryodhana met all situations with negativity. He would consider any success of his cousins as a threat to his position and prestige. When he fell into the water in the palace of illusions, instead of taking it lightly, he took it as a serious humiliation.

After Duryodhana's defeat at the hands of the gandharvas,[9] when he was saved by the Pandavas in exile, he felt so much shame that he initially wanted to kill himself. He was closed to any words of wisdom from the palace elders, taking them instead as personal criticism. He wasn't open to the genuine affection that the Pandavas had for him.

The Pandavas, on the other hand, maintained a helpful outlook. They didn't lose heart when their own cousins tried to kill them, nor did they complain when Dhritarashtra gave them a barren land to rule. Rather, they transformed the wild area into a magnificent kingdom. Even when they were exiled for 12 years, they maintained dignity and courage. As the Sanskrit saying goes:

> *udeti savitā tāmrastāmra evāstameti ca*
> *sampattau ca vipattau ca mahatām ekarūpatā*
>
> The sun is red at the time of rising, and red at the time of setting too. Likewise, great people remain the same at the time of happiness and distress.

Hearing this verse, we might think that a state of perfect equanimity is beyond our reach. However, we can at least try to cultivate a positive outlook in life. Let that be our red sun, in the face of both success and failure. Even if our mind is affected by challenging situations, we can strive to maintain a helpful attitude. If, on the other hand, we see everything through the

---

[9] Celestial beings

lens of negativity, we will lose whatever inner strength we have. Amma says, "Make a firm decision: 'Whatever happens, I will be content. I will be strong. God is always with me.'"

By regularly evaluating our daily interactions and events, we can begin to practice recognizing the difficulties we face, as well as noticing how we can shift our attitudes towards them to be more constructive. It is not possible to change our entire attitude overnight, but we can start with small things.

Once, I was heading back towards my room at night. In those days, my seva[10] was in the kitchen. It had been a long day and the prospect of lying down to sleep was extremely appealing. I suddenly remembered I had forgotten to soak the beans for the next day's breakfast. I sighed, "How annoying! Now I have to go *all* the way back to the kitchen. Otherwise, the beans will take longer to cook and breakfast won't be ready in time tomorrow." I turned around and started retracing my steps. I felt sorry for myself for having to postpone my much anticipated sleep.

I reached the kitchen, measured out the beans, washed them and put them in water. As I walked towards my room, it dawned on me that in all my complaining, I had been seeing the glass as half empty. With a small shift in perspective, I could instead see the same glass as half full. Instead of wallowing in self-pity and grumpiness, I could think how fortunate it was that I remembered the beans at all. Instead of cursing my oversight, I could feel grateful for the timely thought that had saved me a lot of hassle the next morning.

Like this, step by step, we can train ourselves to think in a helpful way in the face of mishaps and difficulties that arise in our daily life. If we are able to develop this skill with regards to the small things, we'll gradually build the mental muscle power to maintain acceptance and equanimity in the face of

---

[10] Selfless service

bigger challenges. Suppose we have to take leave from work to take care of a sick relative. Either we can worry, thinking of the work leave we are using up and our lost income, or we can choose to see the situation as a chance to be present for our loved one, expressing our care and gratitude. By doing this—by seeing the opportunities in even difficult situations—our life becomes balanced and we feel content.

—⌣⌣⌣—

Forgive and Forget

Amma says, "Our efforts to remove hatred and indifference from the world begin by trying to remove them from our own mind."

When I was 12, I had heard and read about Amma but would have to wait another year before receiving her darshan. However, I was fortunate enough to have the few photos I'd seen of her come to life in my dreams. One of those dreams I still remember vividly. It was about a girl at school. In those days, I was friends with more or less everyone in my class, but there was one person whom I just couldn't make myself warm to. I felt judgmental towards her. In my dream, Amma was wearing the same white saree I had seen her wearing in the photos. But there was something different: over the saree, she was wearing a gray coat. I hadn't seen any photos of Amma wearing a gray coat before, but somehow, it looked familiar. When I woke up from the dream, I immediately realized which coat I had seen Amma wearing: It was the coat of the girl in my class whom I didn't like. I felt Amma was showing me that I should let go of my judgments and try to love all. The first step towards this is to shine a torch within, and reveal to ourselves the grudges and judgments we hold.

Amma tells a story about a man complaining to his guru. "There are so many negativities in my mind," he said. "I carry pain from the past, and I can't get rid of it."

The guru gave him a sack of vegetables and told him, "Carry this on your shoulder all the time. Even when you are lying down for resting, keep it on your chest. Do this till I give you further instructions."

The disciple obeyed the guru, carrying the sack at all times. After a few days, the vegetables started to decay and began to stink. As they decomposed further, liquid started dripping all over the man's chest and back. It became repugnant, producing an itchy rash.

Unable to bear the pain and discomfort any longer, he ran to the guru. The guru told him to throw the vegetable sack away, adding, "The burden of your grudges and resentment is painful and unpleasant in your mind. Throw them away just as you did the sack and you will be relieved!"

In reality, forgiveness isn't just something we do for the person who wronged us; it's something we do for ourselves. We are the first ones who suffer from our negative thoughts and emotions. Amma says, "Once we can forgive and forget, peace and happiness will definitely come into our life." How can we gather the maturity and strength to put the bundle down?

We have examples of such greatness of character in our puranas[11] and itihasas;[12] the noble souls depicted there are for us to learn from. There is no point in saying, "Oh, but they were such great mahatmas, they were divine incarnations; I'm an ordinary human being. How can I develop such noble qualities?" No. If such individuals took birth and led their life amongst human beings, we are to see them as beacons who shed a blazing light along the path we need to follow. We can take it step by step and try our best to imbibe a little of the good qualities with which they abound.

Lord Rama's life shows us that we have a lot to learn from each of his relationships. He was a perfect son, a perfect brother,

---

[11] Ancient texts, containing many of the well-known Hindu stories
[12] Written descriptions of important events (main ones are the Ramayana and Mahabharata)

a perfect friend. Let us explore how he was a perfect so-called "enemy" also.

In his debate with Rama in Chitrakoot, Bharata tried all sorts of arguments to convince his brother to come back to Ayodhya and accept the throne. Rama remained firm in his decision to fulfill his father's promise by spending 14 years in the forest. At the same time, he did his best to console Bharata and gave him advice on how to rule the kingdom in his absence. In that context, Rama didn't forget his duty towards even those who considered him in some ways their enemy. Kaikeyi looked upon Rama as a rival to her son, to be gotten rid of by banishment. And yet, in that conversation, Rama told his resentful brother, "Your mother might have done this for you out of fancy or greed. You should not hold it against her. You still have to regard her as a mother."

Seeing the bitter expression on Bharata's face at the mention of his mother, Rama continued, "She did wrong owing to bad motives, it is true. But it would be misguided to harbor ill will against her. Don't hold on to your bitterness. Don't let it brood in your mind. You must behave towards your mother as an ordinary son should." We see here Rama's expansiveness and integrity of character.

We can introspect and identify the negative thoughts we harbor regarding people at work, in our neighborhood, and also in our family. The next step is to reflect on the cost of these resentments to our well-being. Drawing inspiration from Lord Rama, we can try to have the strength and generosity of character to be able to put that bundle down. Even if we have to do this over and over again, we will certainly feel much lighter each time we succeed.

4

Giving and Receiving

According to the Bhagavad Gita, the universe functions on the basis of *yajña*—the spirit of offering. The sun offers its rays and causes clouds to form; clouds offer themselves as rain, rain offers itself enabling plants to grow; plants offer themselves to living beings as food. In this way, all beings offer their contribution at the altar of the macrocosm. The only dissonant element in this cycle is the human being. We depend on receiving for our survival, but our giving is very limited. We give to those we consider our own but tend to be less generous beyond the circle of our family and friends. In truth, it is only through giving wholeheartedly that we are able to enter the natural cycle of life and reach our full potential—achieving a peace and contentment that we might not have thought imaginable before.

The Real Wealth

I have some distant relatives who are extremely wealthy. When I was a child, all our extended family was invited to spend a few days with them. They lived in an enormous and very luxurious mansion. The extensive grounds included a swimming pool and a tennis court. My cousins and I were very excited to spend a few days there; but our parents were worried that we kids might not behave appropriately in such an environment. They exhorted us to be very careful with everything.

The mansion was full of antique furniture, but the attics had been used to store pieces of little value that were no longer in use. Therefore, for unsupervised play time, we would be sent up there in order to stay out of trouble. This seemed like the safest option all round. We wanted to appear well-behaved and not upset anyone. Nonetheless, despite our best intentions, we managed to cause some trouble. One day, as we were playing cards, the youngest of my cousins sat on the edge of a little glass top table, and it cracked.

None of the adults in our family wanted to be the person to inform the owner. Finally, my mother reluctantly agreed to be the bearer of bad news. She explained to him what had happened and apologized deeply for the damage. In fact, in the context of his total material wealth, it was truly insignificant. To my mother's surprise, he was shocked and horrified by the loss. His distress on hearing this story was quite marked. Even as a little girl, I remember being surprised to hear of his reaction. However, on reflection, this is how we are when we become overly attached and identified with external objects no matter how small they may be.

Amma says, "As our attachment towards external objects grows, our mental strength weakens. We may think our attachment is minimal and insignificant. But as our attachment towards an object increases, that object becomes our master." Thinking back, I feel compassion for those relatives. They can't be blamed. They were so focused on their wealth and possessions, they were missing the real wealth in life—the wealth of mutual love, sharing, and giving.

Now let me tell you another story that happened many years later. My brother had been teaching children in a refugee camp. These were children who had been forced to leave their country, had no home of their own, and had often lost or been separated from their family members. My brother was returning home as it was his last day of teaching. When he entered the classroom, he was in for a surprise. The room was decorated with balloons, and there was a pile of goodbye cards for him, drawn by the children. There was a whole feast on the table; every kid had brought some kind of dish. One of the older girls in the class had even baked two cakes for the event. All the children were grinning from ear to ear and looking at my brother, waiting to see his reaction. My brother's eyes filled with tears.

In his words, "Here were children who have been forced to flee their country, who are being robbed of a normal childhood. They have been through so much, have seen such awful things, and have lost loved ones. Yet they were so happy to organize an amazing goodbye party for me. When they saw me crying, they said, 'Sir, don't be sad' and thrust more food into my hands. This just made me cry even more. Then, one of the boys, who is about nine years old, came up to me. He pointed out one of the older girls and explained that she wasn't eating, even though she had spent hours making the cakes. He gave me a piece of cake and asked me to go and give it to her and convince her to eat a bit." My brother told me he couldn't believe the level of consideration and care of this nine-year-old boy.

What a contrast between these two incidents. Although my distant relatives were amongst the richest of people, in a way they were poor. They were missing the basic values that bring real meaning and warmth to life. The refugee kids were extremely poor without even a home or a country to call their own, yet they had the most invaluable of riches. They had the foundation of the basic human values that hold life together.

Amma says, "In our life, selfishness stands as the biggest obstacle to savoring and experiencing joy. We are unable to forget ourselves and love others. We desire everything for ourselves, and we strive to make everything our own. Only when we let go of this mental attitude will joy enrich our lives. Let us let go of our desire to gain from others and foster the desire to give to them. The one who has the mental attitude of a giver is a king. The one who desires only to take is a beggar."

In itself, there is nothing wrong in having wealth, but we should remember it is ours to share with others who are less fortunate. If we focus only on personal gains, we go through life missing the real wealth.

Amma's prayer sums it up: "May the tree of our life be firmly rooted in the soil of love. May good deeds be the leaves on that tree. May words of kindness form its flowers, and may peace be its fruit. Let us grow and unfold as one family united in love."

Circle of Love: Sharing

One day, I was on the terrace of the building where I stay. I was walking up and down while studying. A crow came and landed a few feet away from me. He had a large piece of idli (steamed rice cake, a common breakfast dish in South India) in his beak. I watched him as he ate. After half of it, he must have felt full enough, because he took the remaining piece of idli in his beak and hopped across to where there was a potted plant. He cocked his head from side to side to make sure no one was watching—I guess he didn't see me as a threat!—and proceeded to hide the idli piece inside the plant pot. The plant was bushy enough that his idli was well hidden under its leaves, near its roots.

The crow then flew off. Watching his behavior made me think of us human beings—the tendency we have to accumulate and hoard things. I was intrigued to see what would happen next with our crow. But before he came back, the gardener who owned the plant arrived. In one hand she held a bucket full of cow dung, and a bucket of water in the other. She proceeded to put cow dung and water in every plant pot. Within moments, the idli-piece treasure was buried under a thick layer of dung. As if that wasn't enough, a few moments later it received a full oblation of water. It was gone.

If the crow had called a friend and shared the extra idli, it wouldn't have been wasted. We are often like this crow. We are entangled in our selfishness. Worse yet, we are not just losing a piece of idli. Through our selfishness, we lose out on the very meaning of our human birth.

Amma says, "Each one of us should try to reserve some space for others in our hearts. It is kind hearts that bring about progress in society. If we have just a little love and compassion for others, our selfishness starts fading away and is replaced by a deep sense of fulfillment."

The value of this life is in how much we are able to give and share. If we are stingy with our love and have no time for others, we are the first to suffer. Our joy is in sharing and giving. That is the real expression of life. As says a Sanskrit saying:

dānopabhogarahitā divasā yasya yānti vai
sa lohakārabhastreva śvasannapi na jīvati

The one whose day passes without giving and receiving is one who breathes but has not lived, just like the bellows of the blacksmith.

Once, during Amma's tour of North India, the group of several hundred people traveling with Amma was sitting around her in an open field. We had all finished lunch. After some time, someone handed Amma a packet of biscuits. Amma looked at everyone. "How can I distribute one packet of biscuits to 300 people?" she asked.

Then from the handbags of the householders in the group, one packet came forward, then another, and another... Amma opened each packet and began breaking the biscuits into small pieces with her hands. She filled two or three plates this way, and then had them passed around so that everyone could partake of the prasad.[13]

After making sure we had all received a piece, Amma asked if anyone had any jokes, stories or questions. One of Amma's daughters spoke up. She said how upon seeing Amma go from

---

[13] Blessed offering or gift from a holy person or temple, often in the form of food.

having no biscuits, to having one packet of biscuits to having enough biscuits to feed everyone had reminded her of miraculous tales of food multiplying that we hear about in traditional stories. She said, "So this makes me wonder about the nature of miracles: Is it that something impossible really happens or is it what takes place when we collectively are inspired to give?"

Amma's reply was beautiful: "You cannot create anything that does not already exist in the creation. The greatest miracle is having a mind inclined to share with others."

We need to realize that we have two sides within us. A selfish part—like our selfish crow —that is anxious to keep everything for ourselves and for our family. And also a generous part— one that wants to share with others. It's up to us to decide which part we want to develop and nourish, which part we want to strengthen. Even the smallest bit of effort in cultivating generosity is worth it because it always enhances our well-being.

———⌣⌣⌣———

Real Giving

Dānam (gifting something) is an integral part of Sanatana Dharma. The scriptures provide us with countless examples of great givers, but we can also learn from some of the "counter-examples" depicted there like, the *dānam* of Nachiketas' father Vajashravas, from the Katha Upanishad.

Vajashravas performed a great yaga (ritualistic sacrifice), and as part of that he gave away his entire wealth. His *dānam* was prompted by his desire for the fruit of that yaga, namely attaining higher realms after death and gaining fame on Earth. Nachiketas, his son, was only a small boy. Still, he noticed that his father had kept aside all his valuable possessions for his own family. What he was giving away were only useless and defective things, such as cows that could no longer give milk. Nachiketas had the faith and insight to point this out to his father.

What were the defects of Vajashravas' *dānam*? One, it was based on a selfish motive; he performed it with the expectation of receiving something greater in return. And two, he kept what was of most value for himself, and gave away only objects that he had no difficulty parting with.

If we look within ourselves, aren't there times when we have a similar attitude? When we give, is it not usually accompanied with a hope for recognition? At the very least, don't we expect some love or an expression of gratitude in return? Also, how many of us are willing to give away things that we genuinely value?

Real giving is not only about giving money or material objects. Amma says, "A kind word, a loving glance, a small gesture of help—these alone can make all our lives much brighter. What determines the value of our life is not what we have gained but what we have given. If we gave even one person a moment of consolation, our life would be so much more blessed for it."

There is a couple in Europe whom I've known for a very long time. They are retired, but both remain active in various ways—doing jobs around the house, taking care of their vegetable patch and garden, and volunteering in various ways in their neighborhood. The evenings are their time for relaxing, doing crosswords from the paper, reading a book to each other, or watching TV. Once, when I was staying with them, as soon as we had finished eating dinner, the husband went to put on his wooly scarf and winter coat. Outside was dark—it gets dark very early in the winter in England—and it looked very uninviting. He went out into the cold with a, "See you later!"

I asked his wife where he had gone. She explained: "We have a neighbor. Her husband is in the hospital at the moment. He had a stroke and is in a very bad way. She doesn't drive. So, every morning she takes the bus into the city to spend the day at the hospital with her husband. But there are no buses at night, so we take turns going to fetch her."

I asked her how far the hospital was, and she replied that it was about half an hour's drive. The round trip would take a full hour, every night.

I said, "But isn't that a bit much? Doesn't it use up your relaxing time in the evenings?"

She replied, "Well, a little bit—but we share the same view: If we don't give her a lift, who will? So, we've been doing it. And, you know, at the end of the day, we are happy to do this. It's good to be of help. We feel so sorry for her. She has little money, and her life has been turned upside down."

This felt to me like a true example of *dānam*. Vajashravas had given away only what was of no more use to him, and he had done that expecting special benefits for himself. My friends, however, were giving something that was genuinely valuable to them—their comfortable evening time. And they were doing that without expecting any reward.

Amma says, "The attitude of the person who gives is of utmost importance. When a wealthy man donates for the sake of gaining fame or with some other selfish motive in mind, his donation is degraded into a mere commercial transaction. But when one gives, seeing oneself in others, at personal cost and without expecting anything in return, the results of that giving will be truly great."

In Brihadaranyaka Upanishad, it says:

tad-etat-trayam śikṣed damaṁ dānaṁ dayām iti

Learn these three virtues: self-restraint, giving and compassion for all life. [14]

There is no need for us to feel discouraged thinking about how far we are from the ideal of true *dānam*. But we can try to introspect and become aware of where we stand. We can identify how to improve, how to try to give to others in a genuine way: being generous with what is dear to us and trying not to expect something in return. Recently, a little girl in the ashram told Amma how she had been able to give her favorite toy—a stuffed rabbit—to her friend for her birthday. If this little girl can make little steps in the right direction, we can certainly try too.

———

[14] Brihadaranyaka Upanishad 5.2.3

Fulfillment through Giving

Many of us are unwilling to part with things that are dear to us. At least we can try to be mindful of this and make an effort to change. At the same time, even our imperfect giving is of great value. It enriches our life with a deep sense of fulfillment. Amma says, "The more you give, the more you will have, like an endless spring that flows into the well as you draw water."

I have a friend in the ashram who told me her life's story: "I was brought up in America. I was very athletic as a kid and teenager. As I am tall, I was good at basketball. After my graduation from college, I was taking a trip with some friends. We got into a serious car accident. The car flipped over three times. I was stuck inside a car that had turned into a chapati.

"I had broken my spine in two places and other various bones. I was semi-paralyzed and had to undergo a seven-hour surgery. My neck is held together with two meters of titanium wire and some bone taken from my hip. It was a success. I then began 16 months of full-time rehabilitation. I was in a sort of body cast 24 hours a day and was in constant physical pain.

"My whole world had been turned upside down overnight. Being an athlete, I had always pushed my body to make it perform the way I wanted. Now, I couldn't get up from a chair without somebody helping me. I felt completely betrayed by this body. I also felt cut off from everyone around me. My friends visited me, but they couldn't look me in the eye. I saw that no matter how much my parents loved me, they were completely helpless. They couldn't lessen my pain.

"Questions arose from deep within; questions that I had never asked before. 'What does life mean? What do I want to give back to the world?' Most of the time, I wallowed in feelings of depression and self-pity.

"One day, I got a call from the sports trainer from the school I used to attend. She asked me if I would coach the girls' basketball team. At first I thought she was joking. I could barely move my head from side to side, how in the world would I be able to teach basketball? But she was adamant.

"I was driven to the school and made to sit next to the basketball court. I couldn't show the girls any of the moves. They would gather around me, and I would guide them, explaining what to do. Their youthful enthusiasm brought a ray of hope back into my life. I now had a reason to get up in the morning; I had a gift that I could share with others. I realized that giving this gift was far more rewarding than if I had been able to play basketball myself. This was a huge lesson for me. My feelings of depression and self-pity gave way to joy and fulfillment, even though I could still barely do anything for myself."

Amma says, "Learn to give. Only those who give have the right to take. The one with a mind to give will be welcomed everywhere. What we have taken and experienced will be lost in a moment. What we have given and shared will remain with us forever as contentment, peace, and prosperity."

In the Ramayana, Ravana, the rakshasa[15] king of Lanka, always thought of himself. He never really did anything for others, even those who served him with dedication. He abandoned his own uncle Maricha, forcing him to become a golden deer as part of his plan to kidnap Sita. He didn't care that this would cost Maricha his life. In the battle that took place with Rama and the vanara sena (monkey army), Ravana made so many

---

[15] Demon

rakshasas die, just in the pursuit of his own selfish interest. He didn't even have the consideration to dispose of their bodies in a respectful manner; they were simply thrown into the ocean. He was completely ensnared in his selfishness and negativities.

On the other hand, Lord Rama was all about sharing with others. Because of his consideration, he was loved by all. He offered his deepest heartfelt love and gratitude to Jatayu, who had offered his life in attempting to save Sita. He gave him an elaborate funeral, as he would do for his own father. In the midst of the fight in Lanka, he made sure that the bodies of the monkey soldiers who died were respectfully preserved. They were all revived when Hanuman brought the Sanjeevani plant from the Himalayas. When leaving Lanka in the flying chariot, he invited Vibhishana and his monkey friends to join him in his return to Ayodhya.

The quality of our life depends on how much we share with others, how much we give to the people in our lives. Do we want to be like Rama, or do we want to be like Ravana? The choice is ours. It's not about giving only material help. It's just as much about giving our care, giving our love, giving our time. It is such giving that brings joy to our life and makes our life meaningful. It is in sharing and giving that my friend found a renewed meaning to her life after her devastating accident.

Amma says, "Let us cultivate a mind that desires to give rather than to take. Our existence is based on mutual dependence. Our lives should not be only for ourselves. We are here in this world for only a short while. A butterfly gives great joy to others in its short life span of only a few days. Similarly, our life should be of benefit to others. We must share our wealth and joy with others. We must become one with each other, in mutual dependence and in loving and sharing."

When he visited Amritapuri, the late People's President of India, Dr. APJ Abdul Kalam, said, "I want to share with you what I have learned from Amma: 'Giving.' That is the message I get from Amma. Go on giving. You can give. It's not only money. You can share knowledge. You can remove the pain. And you can even go to the person who is suffering. Every one of us—the rich and poor—can give. There is no greater message than Amma's giving to all the people of this region, and Kerala, and India, and to the world."

An Attitude of Service

Amma says, "What the world needs are people willing to serve, not leaders. Everyone's wish is to become a leader. A real leader is a true servant of people. So, let us learn to serve instead. That is the way to become a real leader."

Draupadi from the Mahabharata was a great queen. At the same time, she was an exemplary servant. In fact, much of the greatness of her character lay in her attitude of service. She always served her five husbands, the Pandavas, with love. She also served Kunti, her mother-in-law, with great care. Her attitude of service wasn't limited to her family members. She was also concerned with providing for the needs of the poor and needy, and about feeding them.

Duryodhana notices this noble quality of Draupadi. After returning from Yudhishthira's *Rājasūya yajña* (a sacrifice cere-mony performed by a king), Duryodhana recounts the events to his father Dhritarashtra. There, he mentions Draupadi:

During this conversation, he mentions what he had observed in Draupadi: "O King, every day of the *yajña*, Draupadi served food to everyone, including those who were physically chal-lenged. Every day, before eating herself, she would take count of how many remained to be fed. Only after they received food would she eat."

Another image of Draupadi's giving and serving nature can be observed by understanding how the Akshaya-patra worked. This was an inexhaustible vessel that fed the Pandavas and their entourage during their years of exile. It was gifted to them by Surya Deva (the sun god). The interesting factor is how it functioned. Every day, it would keep on giving food until Draupadi took her share. So, here too, Draupadi would always place others before herself. She'd ensure that everyone was fed before finally eating herself.

Draupadi drew her strength from her attitude of service. Unfortunately, today, people sometimes consider such an attitude a weakness. Of course, this attitude of service is different from allowing ourselves to become victims of exploitation. And we should also use our discernment to ensure that we are offering our help and service to people who genuinely need it.

Amma says, "We often consider our achievements to be the crowning moments of our life—for example, passing our college exams or receiving recognition in our field of expertise. Although these are significant, there are still greater accomplishments in life. These are found in the little things we do. Consoling someone who's unhappy, helping out those who are struggling—such seemingly trivial things are actually greater than worldly achievements."

In the name of being independent, we run the risk of becoming disconnected from the rest of society and from nature. This attitude can never create a harmonious society. At times, our self-centeredness overshadows our ability to be selfless. We may lose our capacity to empathize with others, to connect and serve others. What we may not realize is that an attitude of service is the best thing we can do for ourselves. It is the way to our own happiness. Our selfishness is the real root of our suffering. Putting others before ourselves is the way to gradually free ourselves from that suffering.

I was feeling sad one day, and I couldn't figure out why. I went about my day feeling down. At one point, a visitor to the ashram approached me and asked me the way to a certain ashram building. She seemed a little distraught. So, after giving her the information she needed, before leaving, I asked her if she was okay. As if she had been just waiting for an opportunity, she started pouring out her heart, telling me the reasons for her distress and the difficulties her family was going through. I spent some time listening to her, trying to be present for her. After she left, I felt concern for her, but at the same time, I was astonished to notice that my own sadness had vanished. Just that act of coming out of my little bubble to tune into someone else's world had pulled me out of my negativity.

Recent research shows a profound connection between altruism and happiness. For example, a new study revealed that executives who gave their bonuses away to help others returned greater happiness scores than those who kept the extra money for themselves. Students given $20 (around 1,500 rupees) in an experiment had higher happiness ratings when they spent the money on someone who needed it rather than on themselves.

Amma says, "The beauty and charm of selfless love and service should not die away from the face of this Earth. The world should know that a life of dedication is possible, that a life inspired by love and service to humanity is possible. In the beginning, just feel inspired by that very ideal. Love the ideal; be inspired by it. In the beginning it is a conscious and deliberate attempt. As you feel more and more inspired by the ideal of selflessness, you start working from your heart. Eventually it will become spontaneous."

———◠◡◠———

5

Stay on Track

Drawing inspiration from a Katha Upanishad verse, Swami Vivekananda famously proclaimed: "Arise, awake, and stop not till the goal is reached." What our scriptures call *lakṣya bodham*, or focus on our goal, is essential for any accomplishment, be it material or spiritual. If we want to be truly goal-focused, we need to gain clarity regarding the skills and qualities we need to develop as well as what habits we need to abandon.

The Pen is in Our Hand

An experiment with dogs was conducted in 1967 at the University of Pennsylvania. The dogs were divided into two groups and then were paired. Each pair was kept in a wooden box with a partition. They couldn't see each other or hear each other. They were then administered small electric shocks that would create unpleasant sensations. One of the dogs had a lever in his part of the enclosure. If he pressed it, the shocks would stop. The other dog didn't have a lever, but his shocks would stop whenever his partner dog pressed his lever. Both received exactly the same number of shocks, but one was in control of stopping them while the other one was not. There was an escape route from the box—one of the side walls was low enough that, with some effort, they could get out.

In all the pairs of dogs, the researchers found the same result: all the dogs that had the shut-off lever were able to then find the way out and escape. Whereas none of the dogs that didn't have the lever could figure out how to escape. The only difference between the dogs was their sense of control. The shocks and the level of difficulty to escape were the same for them all.

The reason the dogs without the lever didn't escape may have been due to their sense of helplessness—a sense that they were just victims of the situation, they had no agency. Whereas the dogs with the lever—empowered by a sense of being able to influence their situation—had the will power and drive required to escape.

Like the dogs in the story, when we realize that we have agency in our lives, we will benefit from a greater sense of well-being and will be more empowered to put in effort towards becoming the person we aspire to be. Whatever external difficulties we face, we have the capacity to choose. Realizing this gives us the confidence to take responsibility and better align our lives to our values.

We sometimes feel like helpless victims. This can dampen our motivation and capacity for action. It may even make us feel a little depressed. Our tendency is to blame the external situation for it. Maybe we feel we are not receiving due love and care from our loved ones. Maybe we feel life is being unfair to us. We may become apathetic and simply complain about our unfortunate situation, possibly blaming our stars or astrological period.

This is where Amma clearly tells us that happiness is always within our grasp. Certainly, we all have essential needs to be met. These include adequate food, shelter, safety and a stable environment during early childhood. Beyond these, what determines our well-being is not so much our external situation, but our attitude towards it. It is important to recognize that our life is in our own hands; our well-being is ultimately our responsibility—no one's else's.

Lord Krishna tells us in the Bhagavad Gita:

> *uddhared-ātmanātmānam nātmānam-avasādayet*
> *ātmaiva hyātmano bandhurātmaiva ripurātmanaḥ*

> Elevate yourself through yourself. Do not lower yourself. For you alone are your own friend and you alone are your own enemy.[16]

Amma gives us a similar message: "We ourselves are the light or darkness in our own path. We ourselves are the thorns or flowers on our path."

---

[16] Bhagavad Gita 6.5

In general, our mind goes on complaining about various aspects of our life: "If only there was better reception for my phone here," "If only the neighbors would stop making so much noise" etc. But the reality is even if one problem gets resolved, the mind will experience only temporary relief. It will swiftly move on to the next issue.

Of course, there are situations that call for efforts at the external level—concrete problems that need concrete solutions. But maintaining a healthy inner attitude is key to being able to be calm and unperturbed whatever the circumstances.

Amma reminds us that trying to fix the external situation, trying to fix the external world, is often like trying to straighten the curly tail of a dog. What we can and should change is our mental attitude. That should be our focus. Amma continues, "Life goes on according to how we write it. We should understand this and not fall into helplessness and depression. During our life there will always be a mixture of pleasure and pain, good times and hard times. Life is like the pendulum of a clock. It swings from challenges to success."

If our life is a story book, ultimately, the pen that writes it is in our hand.

Taming the Monkey Mind

There is a story that Amma often tells: Once a monkey decided to spend a day in meditation and fasting. He sat under a tree and closed his eyes. Immediately a thought came to his mind: "I've never fasted like this before. By the end of the day, I may be too tired even to walk. I could die! If I sit under a fruit tree, then I won't have to go far to find food after I'm done."

He got up and sat under a fruit tree. He resumed his meditation. After a short while, the monkey thought, "After fasting for so long, what if I don't have any energy to climb the tree to get the fruit?"

He climbed up to a branch that had a lot of fruit on it and sat there to meditate. Then he thought, "What if my arms are too weak to pluck the fruits after fasting?" So, he plucked a lot of fruit, held it in his lap and resumed meditating. A little while later, he felt hungry. He thought, "I haven't had such big and tasty fruit in a long time. I can always fast another day!" As soon as this thought entered his mind, the fruit was in his mouth.

Our mind is like this monkey. We want to do certain things, but our mind often doesn't cooperate. It deceives us over and over again. Imagine we want to get up early in the morning to finish an assignment. The alarm goes off, and our monkey mind convinces us: "Just *five* more minutes—there is no harm in sleeping just *five* more minutes." Next thing we know an hour has passed, we have to rush to get ready for work and make up some excuse for not finishing the assignment.

Suppose we love sweets and the doctor has warned us we need to lose weight. We know that we need to eat less sugar and make a firm resolve to stop having it. Suddenly, during the day, the monkey mind speaks up: "Do you remember that box of chocolates you were saving for a special occasion? Their sell-by day may be due soon, and it's wrong to waste food. How about you start your new diet tomorrow?"

The next day, all goes well until we remember that packet of biscuits in the kitchen cabinet. The monkey mind kicks in again: "Ok, well that is a very fancy kind of biscuit. You shouldn't miss out on that. How about you have some of those? And anyway, tomorrow is Ekadashi (traditional day of fasting), so that would be a more auspicious day to start the new diet!"

Like this, our monkey mind keeps cheating us, and we keep being fooled. As a result, we often fail to achieve our goals.

Towards the end of Rama's exile, Ravana kidnapped Sita and took her away to Lanka. Rama was heartbroken, and he and Lakshmana set out in search of her, trying to find some clues as to her whereabouts. As they wandered, they met Sugriva, a monkey king. He was in a sorrowful situation himself. His brother Vali had snatched away his wife and banished him from the kingdom.

Lord Rama and Sugriva became friends, promising to help and support one another. When they met, Lord Hanuman was present. He realized that Sugriva's unstable and flickering mind needed a stabilizing factor to remain loyal to this friendship. Hanuman began to arrange a pit for a sacrificial fire. He lit the sacred fire and orchestrated a ceremony to seal the special friendship.

Clasping each other's hands, the two new friends went around the fire seven times. They took oaths avowing unbreakable commitments toward their friendship. Holding their right hands high over the sacred fire, Rama and Sugriva spoke in unison: "Sealed by this sacred presence of Agni (the fire god), I commit to this bond of friendship." Like this, Hanuman created the ritual sacrifice to help Sugriva's wavering mind stay firm in his commitment to Rama.

Sugriva, the monkey king, represents our monkey mind. And Lord Rama is like our goal. To gain the cooperation of our mind in obtaining our goals we often need a formal commitment. A distracted mind and weak will power block us from tapping into our real potential; this is true in any field in life.

Amma says, "For many of us, our monkey mind will constantly find excuses to avoid doing what needs to be done. We must have determination and a one-pointed focus on our goal. Those who have mental will power and put in sincere effort to fulfill their goals will definitely succeed."

How do we bind our mind to our goals? One good method is to write things down. Amma encourages us to keep a journal. Doing this we are able to clearly identify our goals. It is important to make sure those goals are realistic. As a tip, each day, we can write down only the things that we are confident we should be able to achieve if we keep our mind focused. Only we can be the judge of what a "plausible list" is. We can start with one or two items, and gradually build up from there. At the end of the day, we can check the list and see if we're managing to stay on track. Later, we can take a few minutes to write down how successful we were in achieving those goals. We needn't be disheartened if we've fallen short. Rather we can modify the list the next day to make it more achievable. This will help us develop will power and to conquer the monkey mind. It will empower us to shape our lives the way we want.

———○○○———

Pressing the Pause Button

Once, I was scheduled to give a satsang in the ashram. Three days before the scheduled day, I received a phone call from the swamini in charge telling me that there had been a change of plan, and that my talk had been moved forward to the very next day. At that moment, I agreed, but as soon as I hung up, my mind started freaking out. I thought, "Wait a minute, if I have to give the talk tomorrow, that's in less than a day! It's only in a few hours' time! No way! I need more time to prepare!"

In that moment of stress, I decided to call her back immediately and tell her I actually could not do it. I dialed the number. This was during the first years of the COVID pandemic, and so I was greeted with the familiar audio safety message of that time. I was impatient and wanted to talk to swamini as soon as possible, but instead, I had to wait and listen to: *"Namaskaram. COVID-19 unlock prakriya rajyam embadum arambichu kazhinju. Atu kondu, ningalude vidukalil ninnu atyavashyam undenkil matrame purattu pokavu. Face-cover allenkil mask dharikkumbol, vayum mukkum muzhuvanayi muduvan shraddhikkuka."* (Namaskar, COVID-19 lock-down measures are being lifted across the country. Therefore, only leave the house if necessary. Be sure to fully cover your mouth and nose when wearing a mask.)

I was waiting for the message to end and for the call to get through—that delay created a moment of stillness, a moment of silence. In that moment of awareness, a voice of reason started talking in my head—a sensible voice, a voice of self-confidence. I told myself, "It's okay; I am prepared. I'm just reacting like this because I'm feeling nervous. I should accept the situation and give the talk tomorrow." I canceled the call before it had even started ringing. I felt a keen sense of gratitude towards that corona audio message!

What had happened here? At first, I'd had thoughts of panic and a loss of self-confidence. If I had been able to act immediately upon them, I would have canceled the next day's talk for no valid reason. Instead, that telephone message introduced a little space between my initial thoughts and my actions. That gave me an opportunity to stop and come back to my senses and think before reacting. Because of that moment of awareness, instead of being led by emotions and acting impulsively, I was able to respond in a reasonable way.

Often, we may speak insensitively or act on the spur of the moment, and later we regret it. "If only I had thought a little before doing that..." Amma gives us the tool to rein in our impulsive behavior: "At present, we are unable to keep a time gap between our thoughts and our actions. That is why our thoughts come out as emotional outbursts. If we can create even a small gap between our thoughts and actions, we will gain more control over our emotions." Creating such a gap is like developing an internal pause button. Impulses may be unavoidable, but acting on them isn't. A pause button helps us place a wedge between our impulses and our actions. This allows us to become aware, which in turn gives us the chance to use our discernment and choose the best course of action.

Think about the game of dice between Yudhishthira and Duryodhana. If only Yudhishthira had used such a "pause button"! If he had, there is no way he would have gambled away all his money, jewels, and even his own brothers and wife. Initially, upon entering the royal assembly he had reaffirmed his reluctance to participate in the game. He had mentioned the dangers and negative consequences of gambling. Yudhishthira is considered Dharmaraja, the king of dharma. But even Yudhishthira, when blinded by the frenzy of the game, became unable to create that gap between his thoughts and actions. In the end he even offered himself up as capital, which he then lost. However, in reality, he lost himself much earlier—as soon as he lost that pause button between his thoughts and actions, he lost himself.

If this was the case for someone as established in dharma as Yudhishthira, no wonder we find it so difficult. There are countless times in our life when we lose ourselves. When we react to situations impulsively without using our ability to think carefully and discern, we lose control over ourselves. We become servants of our impulses instead of our mind's master. That is the case when we act in anger, pride, or fear, as I nearly did in the phone-call story.

How do we create that gap, that light of awareness within? How do we press the pause button in the cases when there is no COVID audio message to do it for us? There are many different methods. Each person needs to find the one that works best for themself. It could be doing japa (repeating our mantra) for a few moments. It may be stopping to take a few slow breaths or chanting a prayer or a sacred verse. Such acts may be difficult at first, but if we persevere, that gap between our thoughts and actions will soon begin to arise naturally.

—⬤⬤⬤—

The Judgment of Others

Some behaviors are universal. One is the reaction we have when we fall. Imagine we trip over something in the street and fall down. What will be our first reaction? The first thing we do is look around: "Did anyone see me fall?" Before even thinking about our own physical pain, we are worried about embarrassing ourselves in front of others. Our concern about the judgment of others is deeply entrenched!

Such self-consciousness is an expression of our ego. Amma has pointed out how, despite being committed to the spiritual path, many of us find it very difficult to let go of the ego. In connection to this, Amma usually quotes these lines from a bhajan:

> *mānavum māmūlum lajjayum kḻēśavum*
> *ñān upēkṣikkunna nāḷ varumō?*

> When will that day dawn when I will relinquish pride, archaic conventions, timidity and pain? [17]

Once, when I was at London Heathrow Airport on my way back to India, I was held up for a long time at the check-in counter. As a result, I had only 40 minutes to get from the check-in to the gate. Those who have been to Heathrow Terminal Five know how big and busy a terminal it is and how far it can be to the gates. I ran! The first stop was security; there was a long queue. At last, I got to put my bag on the belt for screening. I ended up being delayed there too because I had forgotten to pull out

[17] Vannālum Ambikē

my iPad. By then, there were only 25 minutes until take-off. I ran again, dodging people on the way. My gate was a couple of shuttle-train stops away. I looked at the time: 15 minutes to go. The train stopped, I took my carry-on suitcase and ran to the escalator.

I started running up the escalator. Probably because I was tired and trembling, my suitcase slipped out of my hand. In shock, as if in slow motion, I saw it sliding down the escalator. I rushed down a couple of steps and swooped down to catch it. I caught it—but fell down onto the steps in the process. By then I was helplessly sprawled on the escalator, my back pushed up against its side. I was trying to get up, but the continuous forward movement of the escalator made it difficult. There were people looking at me, but I didn't care in the slightest. All that mattered was that I made it to the gate.

Panting, heart beating fast, dripping in sweat, I reached the gate. The flight had been delayed, so there was still a queue. As I stood in the queue, the scenes of a few minutes back flashed through my mind. I imagined what I must have looked like to the people coming up on the escalator behind me: collapsed on the moving steps, not getting the balance to stand up. First, I laughed, picturing the scene. Then I started feeling self-conscious. I looked around. Had any of these people seen me fall? Had they witnessed the embarrassing scene?

See what happened here? When I was running, all my attention was on reaching my destination. Therefore, I didn't waste mental energy on anything else. I wasn't at all concerned about what people were thinking of my comical fall. However, when I reached the gate, my focus disappeared. That gave space for self-consciousness and embarrassment. This showed me that if we have a strong focus on a goal, the mental energy we spend on unimportant matters automatically reduces.

When we think too much about how others see us, that means we are lacking a clear sense of purpose. This is true whatever that purpose may be: to chant our mantra and remember the divine, to be mindful of what we are doing, or simply to become a better human being.

In the Bhagavad Gita, Lord Krishna talks of the real devotee—in other words, the one who is truly focused on the supreme. Such a person is *sthira-matiḥ*[18]—"focused on the spiritual goal." It is this very one-pointedness and determination that make him or her unconcerned with the judgment of others: *tulya-nindā-stutiḥ*[19]—"alike in blame and praise" and *samaḥ māna-apamānayoḥ*[20]—"maintaining equanimity in honor and dishonor."

Amma says, "Most of us are very affected by what other people think and say about us. Instead, we should develop self-confidence. If we focus on a higher goal, we will gain the strength to overcome all these mental weaknesses."

———⌣⌣⌣———

---

[18] Bhagavad Gita 12.19
[19] Bhagavad Gita 12.19
[20] Bhagavad Gita 12.18

6

Finding Faith in Ourselves

The scriptures tell us, *tat tvam asi*—"You are that"—your real nature is divine. For most of us, this may seem a little abstract and removed from our daily experience. Developing and nourishing our relationship with God, cultivating love for the divine, using our faith in God to strengthen our faith in ourselves are all steps towards realizing that we are *amṛtasya putrāḥ*—children of immortality.

God as Means or Goal

There was a time before coming to the ashram when it was a priority for me to earn money for flight tickets to follow Amma on her travels. This thought was often at the back of my mind when I interacted with people. Especially with potential "good connections," people I thought could help me find a short-term job. After I moved to the ashram, I didn't have to worry about earning money. I noticed that this shift brought a freshness to my interactions and relationships. I could appreciate people for who they were, without thoughts about what I could get from them.

Our relationships with people can't become rich and fulfilling if our focus is on what we can get out of them. This is also true when it comes to our relationship to the divine. Amma often says, "In general, nowadays people see God as a means, not as a goal. People go to the temple and engage in a sort of bargaining with God: 'I light a lamp for you, and you help me pass the exam. I give you some sweet pudding, and you fulfill my wish.'"

The Srimad Bhagavatam tells the story of Dhruva. His father, king Uttanapada, had two wives, Suruchi and Suniti. Uttanapada had time and affection only for Suruchi and her son. He never spared a moment for Suniti's son, Dhruva. One day, when the boys were both five years old, the king sat Suruchi's son on his lap. Seeing his father playing fondly with his brother, Dhruva innocently tried to climb onto his father's lap as well. But Uttanapada pushed him away roughly.

Queen Suruchi laughed meanly, and told Dhruva, "It's a pity you were born from another woman. You will never climb onto your father's lap, nor onto his throne for that matter. If you want your father's love, pray to Lord Vishnu that in your next birth, may you be born as my son. That is the only way your father will ever love you."

Her words pierced Dhruva's heart, and tears started flowing down his cheeks. His father remained silent. Little Dhruva ran off to his mother; he fell sobbing into her lap. Suniti hugged him and tried her best to comfort him. When she learnt what had happened, she said to Dhruva:

"My child, don't be sad. In a way, what Suruchi said is true. If you want to be a favored son like Uttama, if you want a throne for yourself someday, you must worship Lord Vishnu, the ultimate refuge of all." Dhruva's sobbing subsided. A change came over his young heart. He decided to leave the palace and devote himself to the worship of Lord Vishnu. As he left, Narada (a wandering sage) appeared and tried to dissuade him: "Dhruva, go back home; you are only a child."

But Dhruva didn't waver. He replied, "After what my stepmother said I cannot live there anymore. Besides, my father didn't utter a single word to stop her. My heart is shattered. I want my father's love. Moreover, I want to attain greatness; I want the throne."

Amazed at his determination, sage Narada gave him instructions on how to perform his spiritual practice. He described the enchanting form of Lord Vishnu: his complexion like rain clouds, his brilliant yellow robe, his radiant and gentle presence. Dhruva prostrated and took leave. Narada's eyes filled with tears as he watched the child stride towards the forest on his little legs.

Dhruva performed extreme austerities. He became absorbed in the resplendent form of the Lord. His heart overflowed with love for the dark-complexioned Lord. After six months, Lord Vishnu appeared before the child. Dhruva was on one foot with his eyes closed. He was so absorbed in meditation he didn't realize his beloved Lord was before him. Only when Vishnu withdrew his form from Dhruva's mind did Dhruva open his eyes. Seeing Lord Vishnu, Dhruva chanted his praises, overwhelmed with emotion, tears streaming down his cheeks. He didn't ask for his father's affection, or greatness or throne. Rather, these were his words: "O Infinite Lord, bless me with the company of your great devotees. That way, listening to their stories and songs extolling your glory, my heart will be filled with devotion. I do not want anything else."

Dhruva began his spiritual journey desiring material gains. At the beginning, he viewed God and spiritual practices as a means for getting what he wanted. But this shifted, and God became his goal. Dhruva's love for the Lord deepened; he started loving God for God's sake. His relationship with Lord Vishnu gained indescribable depth and sweetness. When he received the vision of his Lord, Dhruva's life was fulfilled. Moreover, he also received his father's affection and, later, even the throne, as he had wished for initially.

Amma says, "If we ask only for devotion, for love of God, everything else will follow of its own accord. If you catch the queen bee, you catch all the other bees too because they all follow. Similarly, if you love God for God's sake, you will gain everything, without even asking for it." This doesn't mean we shouldn't tell God about our problems. However, as Amma says, "If we tell God about our sorrows, it should be for the sake of getting closer to him."

At times, our attitude towards God may be like my attitude when I was thinking about earning money—seeing others as a means to obtain something I wanted. There is nothing wrong with praying to God for things, but if it stops there our devotion will remain superficial. If we see God as our goal, it will bring about a beautiful transformation in our life—not only spiritually but in all aspects. Everything we need in life will be provided.

Our Inner Witness

I am sometimes quite shy. People usually don't believe me when I say this. I'm not shy talking in front of a camera or in front of a crowd with a microphone. But in certain situations, I am painfully shy. If you don't believe me, you can ask my mum. I remember once she asked me to give a message to our neighbor. I felt so shy I dragged my younger brother along with me.

A few years ago, I had to go and meet someone for advice regarding a project. I had to call him to arrange an appointment. It was someone who I didn't know well and who was senior to me. In general, I don't like calling on the phone, but this time I felt extra nervous. All morning I was fretting about it, telling the people I was working with in the kitchen about how I had to make this phone call.

Finally, I gathered the courage and dialed the number. As soon as I started talking, I realized how unnecessary my tension had been. It was not a big deal after all. We set the appointment time. After the call was over, I felt like a weight had been lifted from my shoulders. I yelled out to my friends in the kitchen: "I did it! I made the call! It's okay, we set an appointment. I'm so relieved!"

Suddenly I noticed my phone. I was on the call! I was confused because I clearly remembered hanging up. Before I could do anything, the call ended. He must have hung up. A few days later, we had the meeting. When it was over, he said, "Immediately after you called the other day, I got another call from you. But all I could hear were some unclear sounds."

I then realized what had happened. After hanging up, my hand must have touched the screen and redialled by mistake. I had been so loud and clear in my triumphant announcement to my friends that there's no way he could have missed it. Luckily for me, he spared me by being polite. Embarrassed, I said, "Oh, really? There must have been something wrong with my phone."

You may laugh—I laughed about it a lot with my friends afterwards—but I'm not telling you this just for entertainment. This incident teaches us a lesson. There are times when we think of God; that may be when we go to the temple or other place of worship, recite archana, or light a lamp in front of an altar. We may talk to God, pouring our heart out, expressing our deepest feelings and wishes. But we may consider that this "conversation" with God is finished the moment we step out of the temple—something we've ticked off our to-do list. However, we do not come "off the line" with God. Because when it comes to our line with God, the line never gets cut.

From our side we may only feel the connection when we are in the temple or puja room, but that connection remains after we step out. That is because God is the *antaryāmī*—the indweller within each of us. God is our *mana-sākṣī*, the witness of our every thought. If we are able to remember that, we will pay more attention to our thoughts. Our devotion will expand—from being just a limited part of our day or week, to pervading every moment of our life. The awareness of God will become part of us. Our every moment will be filled with light.

Amma says, "Our devotion is very limited. We pray and give offerings to God so that he will grant our desires and solve our problems. At other times, we completely forget God. Devotion is not a part-time business. A devotee remembers God at all times and in all circumstances. Similarly, God should be the center point of our life. If so, even in the midst of worldly affairs and our many actions, our attention will be focused on God. This is real devotion."

All Carrying our Burdens

Once, I was carrying a 20-liter water container to the kitchen on my shoulder. I am stubborn; whenever I can, I like to do things myself, without anyone's help. Those water containers are heavy, but as long as I reach the destination fast enough, I can handle it.

But on that day, as I was walking, balancing the container on my shoulder, someone approached me. She had something very important to say. She glanced at the heavy water jar I had on my shoulder, and said, "I suppose I shouldn't really talk to you while you are carrying this, but do you know what happened?" She had been able to talk to Amma about something that meant a lot to her, and she was very excited. She desperately wanted to tell me all about it and thus chose to ignore the fact that I was standing with a 20-liter water container on my shoulder.

I knew how important this was for her, so when she started telling her story, I tried to be an engaged and present listener. But as time went by, the container started to feel heavier and heavier. I could feel my spine compressing under its weight. It became harder and harder to respond enthusiastically. After some time, although I was nodding and trying to smile at everything she was telling me, my only thought was how I could somehow put my burden down.

At that moment, someone walked past us. He saw what was going on and gently reprimanded the lady: "Don't talk to her now. Can't you see she is carrying something heavy?" That instantly brought her to her senses. She said, "Oh, I'm so sorry, I don't know what I was thinking!" I smiled, and before walking on towards the kitchen, I told her not to worry. I didn't want her to feel bad.

Because of my burden, I couldn't be fully present for someone who wanted my attention. But isn't that the state of many of us in life? Often, we are preoccupied with various emotional burdens and worries that weigh us down. As a result, we are unable to enjoy the present moment or be present for others. We live in a state of tension. The solution is simple, yet we often forget it: We have to lay our burdens down. If I really wanted to be present for that person, then I should have found a place to set the container down. Instead, I went on holding it and as such wasn't able to be attentive to the woman's needs.

Amma says, "If we extend our arm and hold a thick book, we may manage to hold it there for five minutes or so. If we force ourselves to hold it like that for an hour, our arm will ache terribly. If we have to hold it the whole day, someone will have to call an ambulance. It is the same way with our sorrows. We need to unburden ourselves of them, leaving them at the feet of the divine through heartfelt prayer. When we pray and offer our worries to the divine, it releases the inner pressure and the mental tension we feel. In fact, it is like a psychological treatment."

Amma gives the example of a man on a train, who carries his suitcase on his head. He suffers and cries that the case is very heavy; he doesn't realize that whether he puts the bag down or keeps it on his head, the train will continue to carry it. Amma says, "This is how our condition is today. We find it so hard to surrender to the divine. In life, we can only put forth our best effort and surrender the rest to divine will. It is in that state of surrender that the Lord accepts all our burdens. Sorrows are our creation—not God's. If we want to be able to face them, then we need to unburden ourselves of them."

The Srimad Bhagavatam recounts Mother Kunti's words to Lord Krishna. She says, "O Krishna, upon the fervent entreaty of Brahman, the Creator, you chose to incarnate among humankind to liberate Mother Earth from the crushing weight that threatened to submerge her, like a ship laden with an unbearable burden."

We also sometimes feel overburdened. What we forget is that the divine is ever present, ready to assume our burdens. An effective and simple way to avail of this is through prayer. All we need to do is turn within and offer our burdens to the divine. Pouring our heart out to the divine is the remedy to relieve us of our sorrows and worries. Remembering that God is our closest relative, we can confide totally in him.

Amma says, "Brooding over the past, anxiety about the future—these are the burdens we all carry. We need to surrender such anxieties at the feet of the divine. If we allow the events of the outer world, whether good or bad, to influence our mind, it will become unsettled and enslaved by sorrow and disappointment. But if we surrender the mind to God, we will always remain calm."

———⌣⌣⌣———

The Divine is Our Strength

Some days the little kids in the ashram get a chance to take the mic and explain their thoughts on various spiritual topics. This is during bhajans, in front of Amma and the whole ashram community. Once, a very small girl came forward, raising her hand. But when she was given the mic, she froze. She was overcome with fear. She forgot whatever she had planned to say, and stood speechless with the mic in her little hand. After trying to coax her to talk, Amma said, "It's okay daughter. Tomorrow bring your mother with you. Let her stand next to you when you get the mic. That way, you will have the courage to talk, knowing her to be by your side." And sure enough, the next day the little girl was able to speak on the mic. The reassuring presence of her mother gave her the courage and confidence she needed.

When Amma talks to the little kids, it is for all of us as well. There are times when we find ourselves in intimidating situations. We may feel we are not up to the challenges that come our way. We lose our confidence; we may panic. We may freeze like the little girl holding the mic. In such moments, a powerful tool to regain confidence and strength is to remember that we are not alone. God is with us. God can't be separate from us because God exists as the true essence within all of us. Amma says again and again, "Never forget that you are not alone on this journey. God is always with you. Allow God to take your hand."

There is an interesting story from the Bhagavatam along these lines. The *daityas* (demonic beings) had defeated the *devas* (gods). Hiranyakashipu, king of the daityas, declared himself to be the god of the whole universe. He strictly enjoined that Lord Vishnu should not be worshiped anywhere. Henceforth, all reverence should be given to Hiranyakashipu alone. Hiranyakashipu had a son, Prahlad. From his very infancy, Prahlad was devoted to Vishnu. His teachers were under strict instructions that the boy should never even hear the name of the Lord. But, from the knowledge and devotion that grew naturally within him, not only did little Prahlad worship Vishnu, but he taught the other boys how to worship the Lord too.

Upon hearing about this, Hiranyakashipu called for Prahlad. Even before his terrifying father, the child declared again and again that Vishnu was the Lord of the universe. The king flew into a rage and ordered the boy to be killed. The daityas struck him with weapons, but Prahlad was so absorbed in thoughts of Vishnu that he felt no pain.

The king then ordered him to be killed through various horrific means. He was trampled by an elephant. But it was to no avail. He was thrown off a cliff. But as Vishnu resided in Prahlad's heart, he came down upon the earth as gently as a flower drops upon the grass. Poison, snakes, fire, starvation, being thrown into a well, black magic—many measures were attempted to destroy the child. None were effective. Nothing could hurt him because Vishnu dwelt in his heart.

At a loss as to what to do, Hiranyakashipu had Prahlad brought to his assembly hall. He asked him, *kaste bala*—"Little one, who is the source of your strength?"

Prahlad's reply is an essential message for us all:

> *balaṁ me vaikuṇṭhas-tava ca jagatāṁ cāpi sa balam*
> *sa eva trailokyaṁ sakalam-iti dhīro'yam-agadhīt*

> Not only for me, but, for you as well as for all this
> world, nay, for all the three worlds, Lord Vishnu is the
> strength.[21]

What gave Prahlad the strength to withstand all the extreme difficulties he suffered? It was his love, determination and firm faith that Lord Vishnu existed within him.

Prahlad, the young devotee of Lord Vishnu, had the absolute conviction that his Lord was ever present—that was his strength. As Amma says, "We exist in God. Every atom is filled with God's presence. To deny God's existence is similar to saying, 'I have no tongue' with our own tongue."

A friend of mine told me of an interaction she had with Amma. During a question-and-answer session in the US, Amma had compared the *jīva* (soul) to a balloon. The *jīva* has to continue to rise up until it attains the goal of life—realizing our oneness with the divine. My friend went up to Amma during darshan and asked, "But Amma, how is my balloon ever going to rise and make it to the goal? I don't know if I have the strength, it is so difficult, and there's so far to go!"

Amma looked at her lovingly and said "My daughter, don't worry. I am the helium in your balloon!"

We all can try taking to heart what Amma told her: We need not worry, because the divine is the helium in our balloon. When Amma says "I," she is not referring to herself as an individual. Amma is referring to the divinity that dwells within every one of us.

In Sanatana Dharma, the sole purpose of the guru is to help us understand who we really are. Amma often reminds us that she is not separate from us. We see a difference because we have yet to realize that we are one with the divine. Amma's Self is the

---

[21] Narayaniyam 24.9

same Self within each of us. It's just that she knows it, whereas we don't. Amma says, "Have faith in yourselves. Have faith in the divine within you." Faith in the guru is sometimes perceived as depending on something external to us. In reality, faith in the guru ultimately brings us to a state of complete independence. It is a tool to help us go beyond our limitations—to go from the small "I" to the all-pervading "I," pure existence. Our bond with the guru takes us to the realization that we are complete and that the guru—the divine—was within us all along.

Amma says, "We should try to have the faith that God is always with us. This awareness will give us the energy and enthusiasm that we need to transcend any obstacle in life. This optimistic attitude should never leave us."

———◯◯◯———

The Treasure of Loving God

As kids, we are told not to play too much, as our homework will suffer. If we love art or music, we are advised to also focus on something more practical. If we love to travel, we are told not to do it too much; we also have to settle down and get a job and family, etc. We enjoy ice cream, but if we eat too much, we will get sick. It's good to love people, but we need to be careful not to get too attached or we might suffer later on. All this may be true. But there is one area in life in which we can freely, fully, fearlessly give ourselves with abandon. We find it as a common thread in the writings of mystics from all religious traditions. It is the most precious thing in life. It gives so much joy that all other joys fade in comparison. What is it? It is love for the divine—love for God.

Amma says, "Whatever falls into sugar becomes sweet. Similarly, because God is bliss, our closeness to God gives us bliss. Take refuge in God, and all spiritual and material gains will be yours."

We all have a spark of love for God within us because God is our true nature. It isn't restricted to love for a formal representation of God. Love for God may manifest as devotion towards the divine in the form of nature or in the form of beauty or in the form of compassion. We may feel the touch of the transcendental while listening to a beautiful piece of music or spending time in nature. Our love for God is an expression of our desire to know our real essence—our desire to know ourselves. It is an expression of our longing to return to our source. We may experience only occasional glimpses of these manifestations of the divine, but we can try to fan the spark. Here, there can be no overdose, and there are no harmful side effects.

When love for God becomes our center, every aspect of our life gets enhanced. That's what Amma indicates when she says that all material gains will be ours if we place our trust in God. The expression of our bond with the divine is twofold. The first aspect is *pūjā-manobhava*—performing all our actions with an attitude of worship. The second aspect is *prasāda-buddhi*—accepting what comes to us as coming from God. Together, these two shifts in outlook make us better at everything we do—at all the roles we play. We will be a better friend, a better parent, a better son or daughter. We become a better nurse, businessperson, teacher, cleaner or engineer. That love will be expressed through everything we do, bringing fulfillment and beauty to our lives.

How do we place love for God at the center of our life? We can learn from Shabari,[22] the great devotee of Lord Rama.

As they were wandering through the forest in their search for Sita, Rama and Lakshmana came across a small hermitage nestled in the forest. There, they were greeted by Shabari, who garlanded them and knelt at Rama's feet, tears streaming down her cheeks. The brothers sat on grass mats she had neatly laid down for them. Shabari lovingly placed a leaf plate of fruits before Rama and Lakshmana. The hermitage was swept impeccably clean. It was decorated with many different kinds of flowers, and a delightful fragrance permeated the air.

Why was it that Shabari had prepared for Rama's arrival? Her guru, Matanga Rishi, before leaving his body, had told her that one day, Lord Rama would come. "You wait here," he said. "Rama will come and visit your little hut! Serve him with great love."

---

[22] Shabari was from a tribe of forest dwellers

Though he had said Rama would come, he had not said when. For 13 years, Shabari expected Rama to come any day, at any time. For 13 years, every day she cleaned the hermitage spotlessly, thinking of Rama's comfort. Every day, she would lovingly sweep the path to the hut's entrance. Every day, she would fetch the best flowers; she would make beautiful garlands for Rama and decorate the hut. Every day, she would gather the best fruits and berries, knowing that it would be her chance to feed him with her own hands. Every night, Shabari would lie down on the floor with the words of her guru ringing in her ears—"Rama will come! Serve him with love."

Her immense love inspired her to keep on waiting, with no idea how long the wait would last. Now, with tears streaming down her cheeks, Shabari gazed at her Lord's radiant face, drinking in his beauty; her life had been fulfilled.

During the 13 years of waiting, Shabari's every movement became an act of worship. That's why there was such perfection in her actions. We too can bring beauty and grace into our actions. For this Amma teaches us to do everything with a *pūjā-manobhāva*—an attitude of worship.

In Amma's own words, "Love is a *mahā-mantra*. It is a mantra that gives one the strength to face any kind of challenge. But it is not a mantra to be chanted with the lips. It must be chanted with the heart."

We can't transform our heart into a most beautiful temple overnight; but we can build it up gradually, step by step. We can try to orient our minds towards the divine. In this, no effort is lost; every action of love, every action of compassion is one more stone laid in the building of our temple. Every mantra, every moment of mindfulness, every prayer is a flower placed before the shrine.

Amma says, "Your heart is the real temple. You must install God there. Good thoughts are the flowers to be offered; good actions are worship; good words are hymns. Love is the divine offering."

7

Following Nature's Lead

According to Sanatana Dharma, the universe functions on the basis of *yajña*—the spirit of offering. In other words, animals, human beings, plants—all entities in creation—are integral parts of the whole. Thus, the balance and harmony of the macrocosm depends on the mutual cooperation of all the constituent microcosmic parts. This principle is also referenced in deep ecology philosophy. It speaks of the idea that nature is not simply a resource to be used by humans but has an inherent worth that must be honored. At present, we human beings are the dissonant element in this cycle of reciprocal giving and receiving. The way forward has to be a profound shift in our attitude towards nature and in how we treat her.

Nature, Our Mother

We are familiar with Sita's story. She was born directly from the Earth. King Janaka found her in a furrow, while he was plowing a field as part of a Vedic ritual. At the end of the Ramayana, we see her return to Mother Earth. Sita prays, *me mādhavī devī vivaraṁ dātum arhati*—"May the Earth-Goddess grant space to me."[23] The Earth-Goddess appears, and welcomes Sita, taking her by the hand and greeting her with words of welcome.

We need to remember that Sita is not the only daughter of Mother Earth; in reality, every one of us is her child. Amma says, "Nature is our first mother. She nurtures us throughout our lives. Our birth mother may allow us to sit on her lap for a couple of years, but Mother Nature patiently bears our weight for our entire lives. She sings us to sleep, feeds us and caresses us."

It is well known in psychology that if a child is separated from its mother at an early age, there is emotional damage—a sense of incompleteness, a sense of loss. There is a similar sense of incompleteness within us because we have forgotten our deep connection to nature. We may not realize it because we have completely forgotten that we are part of nature. This reinforces our feeling of isolation. As Amma says, "We are not isolated islands; we are all links in a chain. And that chain doesn't only connect us to other human beings. It connects us to the whole universe."

---

[23] Ramayana, Uttarakanda 97.14

When my grandmother was diagnosed with MND (motor neuron disease), the whole family was devastated. The condition progressed, and within two or three years, she needed more support. Along with my grandfather, they moved to a flat in a residence for elderly people, where there was wheelchair access. This was a challenging time for my grandfather; he was my grandmother's primary caregiver. He helped her as best he could in all her daily activities. After some time, he started feeling quite physically drained and emotionally down. The challenge of tending to his wife's needs and trying to come to terms with the idea of losing her started taking its toll.

One day, he noticed the churchyard just down the street. He had an idea. He went to a gardening shop and bought some flower bulbs. He selected bulbs for purple, orange and white crocuses that would be colorful but at the same time blend nicely with the wildlife at the churchyard. The very next day, he started his work. He went to the yard and got on his knees—his 80-year-old knees—and started planting. He poured himself into his new gardening project. He could only be away from my grandmother for a short time, but he made it a point to go daily and loved every moment he spent working with earth and planting the bulbs. It took a long time because he literally planted hundreds of them. After a few months, shoots started coming up. Soon the flowers started blooming, to his great joy and to the appreciation of passersby.

The time my grandfather spent in his new little garden reinvigorated him. He'd return to my grandmother with renewed enthusiasm. The connection he felt to nature, through digging the soil, planting the bulbs, and caring for them, helped him to maintain a positive attitude during that difficult time.

Once I was talking to an ashram resident who works at one of our gardens. She told me they'd often go to Amma for guidance regarding their seva. Amma's most frequent piece of advice to them was to love the plants. Amma often tells us, "Kiss the plants, talk to them." Not only do the plants benefit from those vibrations of love, so do we. Our heart opens to nature. This is a way for us to remind ourselves of our bond with nature.

Amma says, "When we human beings fall in love with nature, she falls in love with us. She will stop hiding things from us. Opening her infinite treasure of wealth, she will allow us to enjoy her. Like a mother, she will protect, nurture and nourish us. Look at the beauty of nature. Living harmoniously with nature in itself brings us happiness and contentment."

The principal of one of the ashram's primary schools told me that she had all the children plant a sapling and give their saplings a name. Each morning, the children were taught to water their plants and circumambulate them with reverence. On the last day of school before the holidays, she overheard several of the children talking to their particular plant: "During vacation, I won't be here to water you. But don't be sad. I will come back in two months. Don't cry." No one instructed them to do this; it was the spontaneous expression of the bond they felt with their plants. The simple act of planting a sapling gave those children a genuine sense of connection with nature.

We can plant some vegetables and trees. If we don't have a garden, we can at least keep a single plant in a pot in our home. We can encourage our children to spend time outside, let them enjoy running barefoot in the sand and playing in the rain. Even if we live in the city, we can seek out the nature present there, amidst the city bustle. We can keep some seeds and water on our window ledge for birds.

Through trying to kindle our bond with nature we can come to profoundly experience the Vedic truth, *mātā bhūmiḥ putro'ham pṛthivyāḥ*—"The Earth is my mother, and I am her child."[24]

Nature's Perseverance

The world has been stumbling from one crisis to another. We've experienced a global pandemic, economic uncertainty, conflict, political and social turmoil, and natural disasters. And of course, there are also personal traumas, such as losing a loved one, declining health, unemployment, divorce, violent crime, and tragic accidents. Whether the source of disruption in our life is a global emergency or a personal tragedy—or both—living through difficult times can take a heavy toll on our well-being. How do we maintain our strength and courage in such tough situations? How do we remain optimistic when it sometimes seems like there's no light at the end of the tunnel?

Amma says, "Nature is a textbook from which we must learn. Each object in nature is a page of the textbook. Every object in nature teaches us something." Let's turn to nature for some lessons about persevering and not losing hope.

Once, near the ashram kitchen, a friend planted two banana plants. After a week, a green shoot appeared out of the ground. I started checking on it every day and was amazed at how fast it grew. A week later, it was almost a foot tall! Then, one day, I noticed a green shoot coming forth from the second plant. I thought that my family would be impressed seeing how fast it grew. There are no banana plants in England, and in general plants grow much slower there.

I started sending them a weekly photo of this second banana sapling. They enjoyed watching its progress. But after a few weeks, when I looked at the plant, it was crawling with ants. From then on, its growth was stunted. It seemed like it was trying to fight back—and at least it wasn't dying—but it had stopped growing. My friend tried all sorts of things to drive the ants away. She moved it to another place and noticed that it had barely developed any roots. She put turmeric powder around it to deter the ants, but no matter what she did, they kept coming back with their vehement attacks.

She wasn't very hopeful the sapling would survive. I stopped sending my family updates. I didn't want to tell them disappointing news when the world situation was grim enough already with the COVID pandemic. Months went by, and the little banana sapling remained at the same height—maybe one foot. Its few leaves were yellowish and withered. Meanwhile, its older sister had grown almost as tall as me.

Suddenly, one day, we noticed a new, strong, green leaf shooting up. The little plant had made it. It started growing again. It grew into a healthy plant—its vigorous green leaves stretching up towards the sky. We were all delighted. What a lesson the plant was teaching us! A lesson of perseverance, a lesson of hope. Needless to say, I started sending photo updates to my family again. Amma says, "Life is filled with God's light, but only through optimism will you experience that light. Look at the optimism of nature. Nothing can stop it. Every aspect of nature tirelessly contributes its share to life. The participation of a little bird, an animal, a tree or a flower is always complete. No matter what the hardships, they continue to try wholeheartedly."

Let me share another small incident. As part of a plan to extend the ashram kitchen, we needed to put a tin roof over an open area. In that area was a tree. Amma was adamant the tree should not be cut. So, the metal sheet was built around the tree. A hole was made in it for the big trunk to go through. Most of the tree's branches were high up, well above the metal sheet. But we had to cut its lower branches in the process.

What happened in the next few months became a source of inspiration for all of us in the kitchen. Naturally, the higher branches of the tree, the ones above the metal roof, continued growing. But the tree also grew two new branches under the corrugated iron sheet—basically, inside the kitchen storage area. Those branches didn't receive any direct sunlight, but they burst forth with vibrant green leaves. Every morning when I'd arrive for my kitchen shift, I would be greeted with their message of hope.

Another small anecdote that shares a lesson from nature comes from the days when I worked in the kitchen. One of my tasks was to sprout the mung beans. Every day, before soaking the beans I would sort through them, checking for broken ones and stones. One morning, when I removed the lid covering the sprouts, I saw a broken bean that I had missed the previous day. I picked it up and was amazed at what I saw: it was only half a bean, but it had developed a sprout that looked just as healthy as that of the whole beans. A small bean can grow into a plant, even if it is cracked or damaged—isn't that a lesson for us, to stay hopeful even when our life may seem broken?

Amma says, "See how easily nature overcomes obstacles. If there is a stone in the path of a tiny ant, the ant just walks around the stone and continues on its way. If there is a rock where a tree is growing, the tree simply grows around the rock. In the same way, a river flows around a log that is blocking its path. We, too, should learn to adapt to all circumstances in life, overcoming them with patience and enthusiasm."

chinnopi rohati taruḥ kṣīṇopyupacīyate punaścandraḥ
iti vimṛśantaḥ santaḥ santapyante na viplutā loke

> A tree, though cut down, grows again; the moon, though waned, waxes again; taking this into consideration, the wise are not troubled in this world when in times of hardship. [25]

During difficult times, a message that Amma tells her devotees across the world over and over again is, "Don't lose courage, don't lose courage." Drawing inspiration from nature, we can learn how to remain courageous. We can learn from the little banana sapling that kept persevering through those months of ant attacks. We can learn from the kitchen tree that grew new branches and leaves even after losing several branches and its exposure to sunlight. We can learn from the broken mung bean that was able to germinate. As Amma says, "Victory is assured where there is hope and effort."

---

[25] Bhartrihari Nitishatakam

Honoring Nature

It was the rainy season in Vrindavan. The villagers planned to perform a *yajña* (sacrifice ritual) to please Indra, the king of gods. They cleaned the whole village and decorated it with lights and flowers. Seeing all the commotion, little Krishna asked his father, Nanda: "Father, what do you hope to gain from the *yajña*? Which deva (god) do you mean to worship?"

Nanda replied, "Indra is the lord of the rain, the master of the clouds. We have to please him through our *yajña*. If there is no rain, our land will be dry and our fields barren."

Little Krishna objected, "No, Father, it's not Lord Indra but the Govardhana Mountain that is our friend and well-wisher. It's him we should thank."

Many villagers had gathered around. Krishna continued emphatically: "The mountain interacts with the clouds to make rains fall over Vrindavan. It is the mountain that gives us medicinal herbs and purifies our water. It provides good healthy grass for our cows, by which we get nutritious milk. Our lives depend so much on the mountain. I say you should perform the *yajña* not to honor Indra, but to honor our cows and the great Mount Govardhana."

Krishna's instructions were enthusiastically followed by the villagers. With love and faith, they offered all sorts of delicacies to the mountain, in accordance with the traditional methods of worship. Krishna lay down before Govardhana Mountain in full prostration; the villagers followed him. Then, they returned to their homes, their hearts full and content.

Seeing the villagers worshiping the mountain instead of him, Indra became enraged. He called terrible clouds of devastation and ordered them to lash torrents of rain and thunderstorms upon Vrindavan. Thunder and lightning tore through the sky. Rain fell in torrents. Terrified and drenched, all the villagers and animals gathered around their only refuge, their only hope—Krishna. Swiftly, Lord Krishna lifted the entire mountain. He increased his size and held the mountain up gracefully, as an elephant holds a lotus flower with his trunk. He then called out, "Father Nanda, Mother Yashoda, all the people of Vrindavan! Bring your children and your herds with you, come under the mountain and take shelter from the storm!"

The cowherds loaded their carts with all their possessions. Bringing their families and their animals with them, they came, one by one, into the safe sanctuary. For seven days and nights, Indra's storm raged all around them. But it was to no avail; all the inhabitants of Vrindavan were safe beneath Govardhana Mountain. At last, Indra recognised Krishna's divinity. He admitted defeat and left, withdrawing his clouds.

Within moments, the rain stopped, and the sky became clear. The sun shone again. The strong winds fell still. Krishna said to the cowherds, "Come out now, my people. There is nothing left to fear." The villagers all emerged from under the mountain. Not only people, but also cows, deer, squirrels, goats, birds—all sorts of creatures had taken refuge in the sanctuary of Krishna's protection. Everyone sang and danced in celebration, overwhelmed with joy and love for their young cowherd.

This story is highly significant, especially today when people have very little love and reverence for nature. By worshiping Mount Govardhana, Krishna gave us a profound message. He showed us that God's presence shines in and through every single aspect of nature, such as mountains, rivers, trees, plants, flowers and animals. Therefore, to worship God, we should honor and take care of nature. We need to remember how completely dependent we are upon nature.

Amma says, "The air we breathe, the water we drink, the food we eat, the home in which we sleep, the sun that gives us energy—we are indebted to nature for all of these. Our life on this earth is possible only because of the combined effort of all its creatures. The rivers, trees, bees, butterflies and worms all play their part. If they did not exist, we would not exist. There would be no life."

Amma continues, "Along with our efforts to protect and preserve nature, we should also develop love and reverence for nature. Our ancestors worshiped forces of nature, even poisonous snakes."

In the 1980s, due to indiscriminate felling of trees, Attappadi, in Kerala,[26] became completely barren. Pained by seeing the tragedy of the region, poetess Sugathakumari and a few others decided to reforest a hill in the area. They named it Krishna-vanam. Volunteers and tribal people, working side-by-side, planted one sapling at a time. Today, Krishnavanam is bursting with greenery and wildlife. It is a testimony of the potential of human effort—the initiative of one or two people inspired others. All the individual efforts came together to bring about a remarkable change.

How can we cultivate a respectful and prayerful attitude towards nature and translate it into our actions? One point Amma stresses is the importance of teaching children to love and respect nature. We can also try to develop awareness regarding our use of natural resources, trying to use only what we need. We can try to remember to have gratitude for what we receive from nature. We may feel that our little effort is

---

[26] Palakkad District

insignificant. But it is not. If we stand together, all of our little efforts can combine to bring about change. Seeing our actions may inspire others to join in too—just like how the villagers of Vrindavan joined in with Krishna in bowing before the Govardhana Mountain.

Amma says, "Nature is an indispensable part of life on Earth. Everything relies on nature to live. We are not different from nature; we are an interdependent part of her. Our lives depend on the well-being of the whole. Therefore, it is one of our foremost duties to lovingly care for all living things. Nature is God's visible form that we can see and experience through our senses. By loving and serving nature, we are worshiping God directly. Let us try to reawaken this attitude."

The Real Ahimsa (Non-Violence)

The following words were spoken by Bhishma to Yudhishthira, after the Mahabharata War:

ahiṁsā paramo yajñaḥ tathāhiṁsā paramaṁ balam
ahiṁsā paramaṁ mitram ahiṁsā paramam sukham

Ahimsa is the highest sacrifice; ahimsa is the greatest strength. Ahimsa is the best friend, and ahimsa is the greatest happiness.[27]

I've always considered myself someone who practices ahimsa. I love animals and birds. I often walk up and down on the terrace of the building where I live and enjoy watching the crows. Each one has its own personality and character. But one day, a crow swooped down very close and pushed down on my head before flying away again. I was totally taken by surprise. It was very clear that this was an act of protest—like he wasn't happy because I was in "his" area. He perched on the railing nearby. I looked at him in shock. "Don't you understand I'm a friend, not a foe?"

I thought about it. I thought about how Amma is with animals, and realized that my ahimsa isn't real ahimsa. In reality, the kind feeling we have towards animals and birds is shallow because our worldview is one in which animals are distinct from us. Everyone's worldview is egocentric, and our sense of "I" stops with our own body and mind. There is us, and there is the rest of the world. The sense of "I," the ego, stands as a barrier.

---

[27] These words are spoken by Bhishma to Yudhishthira, in the Mahabharata.

Therefore, the love we feel for other beings is limited; the "I" always comes first. That "I" always holds the central position in our individual worlds. Whereas it is entirely different for Amma. Amma embodies the highest ideal of ahimsa because she sees the entire creation, with all its birds, animals and plants, as part of herself. There is no barrier or separation.

Amma says, "A person who has become one with the supreme consciousness sees nature as God. They don't experience nature as being separate. They are the real lovers of nature. When there is no mind or ego, you are one with the whole of existence. When you are one with creation—when your heart is filled with nothing but love—all of nature will be your friend and will serve you. The universe, along with all of its beings, is your friend."

These words are reflected in all of Amma's actions. We can see this in her interactions with animals and birds. This reminds me of an incident a friend of mine told me about. It was during Amma's US tour. He was standing next to Amma's darshan[28] chair, translating the questions of the devotees. At one point, he noticed that Amma had paused the darshan. She was carefully picking something off a flower someone had given her. My friend leaned closer to see. Amma showed him a little insect that was now on her hand. She then placed the creature on a piece of tissue paper. Amma proceeded to carefully fold the tissue paper around it, giving it a cushioned protection. When she had finished wrapping it up, Amma gently handed the little folded bundle to my friend. She said, "Son, go and release it outside, next to some plants. If you put it somewhere close by, hopefully it'll be able to rejoin its family members."

---

[28] In Amma's case, darshan is the individual embrace she gives to those who come to meet her.

As he carried out the task, he was humbled by Amma's compassion towards all creatures. With what care and attention had she wrapped up the little creature, that too in the midst of a busy darshan! The way Amma cared for the insect that day is evocative of a verse in the Srimad Bhagavatam:

> *mṛgoṣṭra-khara-markākhu-sarīsṛp-khaga-makṣikāḥ*
> *ātmanaḥ putravat paśyet taireṣām antaraṁ kiyat*

> One should consider animals such as deer, camels, donkeys, monkeys, mice, snakes, birds and flies as one's own child. What difference is there between these creatures and one's own offspring?[29]

A long-term ashram resident from Tamil Nadu, now in her 80s, told me how first thing every morning her mother would draw a *kōlam* in front of the entrance to their house. A *kōlam* is a form of decorative art that in those days was drawn using rice flour. Its geometrical design is supposed to welcome Lakshmi (the Goddess of Prosperity) and drive away evil spirits. Nowadays people draw such designs using stone or chalk powder. The tradition of using rice flour not only beautifies the entrance to one's home, but it also is a food offering to ants and other little creatures. The now elderly lady remembers watching as a child, as the ants would come and partake of the offering. Her mother was skilled at drawing intricate designs. Every morning she would sweep away whatever was left of the previous day's *kōlam* before drawing a fresh new pattern. The designs would be even more elaborate during festivals. In Sanatana Dharma, this morning offering is part of *bhūta-yajña*—the ritual of feeding animals, birds and insects.

---

[29] Srimad Bhagavatam 7.14.9

Amma says, "We must remember that everything is sentient. Everything is full of consciousness and life. Everything exists in God. There is no such thing as "mere matter." Consciousness alone exists. Ages ago, the saints and sages of India, having understood this great truth, lived a life of perfect ahimsa."

The World as Our Garden

In January 2013, we were traveling with Amma on her tour of India. It had been two months of a fast-paced tour. Large crowds, never-ending darshans, long bus rides... We were at the last stop—Calcutta. Amma came for the usual program of satsang,[30] bhajan,[31] meditation and of course, darshan. It was towards the end of the program when Amma had been giving darshan for 12 hours:

I was sitting on a chair, struggling to stay awake. It had been a long day. I was waiting to see Amma leave and looking forward to getting some sleep after that. But soon, I realized Amma had a different plan. There was some commotion in the back of the hall. "Do you know what is happening back there?" I asked the person sitting next to me. "Didn't you hear? After darshan Amma is going to go and clean the road that runs past the ashram. You'd better be ready; we are all going with her!"

Sure enough, the commotion at the back of the hall was people distributing supplies for the cleaning party. Rakes, shovels, gloves, masks, and sacks to collect the waste.

When the last person in line had received darshan, Amma came down from the stage. She walked straight out of the ashram to the road outside. The enthusiasm in the atmosphere was so contagious that I was shaken out of my sleepiness. We all followed Amma eagerly, empty sacks in hand.

---

30 Spiritual talk
31 Devotional singing

Amma put on gloves and a mask and got right into the filth that had accumulated over the years along the roadside. Then, for the next three hours, about 800 devotees joined Amma in cleaning three kilometers of roadside. It was a real festival—a festival of picking up garbage of all shapes and sizes and smells.

At the end, a large lorry arrived to collect all the bags of trash we had collected and kept along the side of the road. Throughout the night, many of the ashram's neighbors were roused from sleep by the sounds of laughter and joy. We saw several stunned faces! Think of their surprise when they realized the unusual celebration taking place outside in the cold night was that of complete strangers from all over the world cleaning their neighborhood! The next morning, we set off on the long journey back to Kerala. We all enjoyed seeing in daylight the result of the night's work. The road was spotless. This is Amma's greatness. This is what people mean when they say she "walks the talk." What better way is there to teach than through your own example?

Connected to this, there is an anecdote about a little girl who lives in America in Amma's Chicago ashram. She has a very special bond with Amma and takes Amma's teachings very much to heart. Once, she was with her parents at Amma's program in Detroit. She wasn't even two years old at that time. Amma was on the way from her room to the hall. She called the little girl into the elevator with her. In the elevator, the girl noticed a piece of rubbish on the floor. She said, "Ooh!" and pointed at it to Amma. She then proceeded to bend down to pick it up. It was a candy wrapper, and it was a little stuck to the floor. But the little girl wasn't going to leave it there. She was adamant it had to be thrown away. Amma watched her with delight and said, "See, she can hardly walk or talk, but she is so concerned about Mother Nature! She knows that rubbish needs to be disposed of correctly!"

Amma was so impressed seeing the little girl's love for nature and her awareness of dharma that the next day she told everyone about the incident.

Amma says, "As soon as we wake up in the morning, we brush our teeth. Environmental cleanliness is just like that. It's for our own health and well-being."

The relationship between humanity and Nature has lost its harmony. We need to strive to rebuild it. Some people may ask, "What difference does picking up some trash do?" But in reality, this is very significant. Pollution through the irresponsible disposal of waste is a very real problem. But almost more importantly, cleaning up helps shift our perspective. Each time we engage in such activities, it helps cement within us the awareness of our responsibility in the well-being of the Earth.

Rather than limiting our home to the four walls of our house or to the fence around our land, we need to expand our vision to see the whole world as our home. And when we try to clean up our environment, we make it nicer for everyone. In this way, no effort is insignificant. Every action is a step towards building a harmonious relationship with nature—our collective home.

Amma says, "We may doubt whether we have the power to restore the lost balance in nature. We may ask, 'Aren't we human beings too limited?' No, we are not. We have infinite power within us, but we are fast asleep and unaware of our own strength. This power will rise up when we awaken within."

What can we do? We can start from our home. At least we can try reducing the waste we generate. Let's put in the effort to sort and recycle it. Inspired by Amma's example, we can put in efforts to keep our neighborhood clean. Together, step by step, let us rebuild a harmonious relationship with our common environment.

8

Listening and Speaking from the Heart

Our experience in the world is defined, to a significant extent, by how we interact with others. Sometimes our listening—whether to others or to spiritual teachings—is half-hearted or distracted. Sometimes we speak without sensitivity and awareness. The remedy to both of these is to try to listen and talk from the heart. If we can be present, humble, open and loving when we communicate, all our interactions become opportunities for us to grow.

Śravaṇam—Receiving Wisdom

Even after the Pandavas finished their period of exile, the Kauravas refused to return their kingdom, Indraprastha, to them. Krishna was sent as a messenger to the Kuru court at Hastinapura. It was a final attempt to make king Dhritarashtra understand the importance of peace.

Lord Krishna's only intention was to bring about peace and the welfare of all. He was welcomed to Hastinapura with great pomp. Krishna addressed the assembly, and spoke from compassion and love. He warned the Kauravas of the terrible destruction that would occur in the absence of a peaceful agreement. He urged Duryodhana to strike a compromise with the Pandavas who were eager to make peace.

He told Duryodhana, "If you make peace with your cousins, Yudhishthira will make you crown-prince of Hastinapura. And after your father's time, you will rule as the king of the Kurus. The Pandavas will be content with Indraprastha and will never be a danger to you. With your cousins on your side, you'll have such power that none will dare challenge you. Act with nobility and you will become king, making this age one of the brightest the world has seen. The future of the world is in your hands." After Krishna, Bhishma then addressed Duryodhana: "Krishna has spoken words of a friend wishing for peace; listen to him, my dear son."

But Duryodhana was unable to listen. He was unable to receive Krishna's words with his heart. He was closed and remained firm in his selfishness and his hatred towards the Pandavas. His failure to listen and receive the sage advice given to him had devastating consequences. Ultimately, it led to the very destructive Mahabharata War.

Bhartrihari, a famous philosopher, grammarian and poet, in one of his poems the Nitishatakam, created a beautiful image:

santaptāyasi saṁsthitasya payaso nāmāpi na śrūyate
muktākāratayā tadeva nalinīpatrasthitaṁ rājate
antassāgaraśuktimadhya patitaṁ tanmauktikaṁ jāyate

Water evaporates completely when it falls on a heated iron plate. If it falls on a lotus-leaf, it shines, resembling a pearl. When it falls into an oyster in the ocean it becomes a pearl.[32]

This comparison illustrates well the three different kinds of *śravaṇam* (receiving wisdom). The first kind of *śravaṇam* is compared to a dosa[33] pan. The pan is heated, and when water is sprinkled on it, the water immediately evaporates. Some people are like a dosa pan—hot with their arrogance, hot with their prejudgments. When the guru's soothing words fall on their ears, they have no effect. They evaporate immediately—"In one ear, out the other." This was how Duryodhana received Krishna's words.

The second way of receiving spiritual wisdom is like a dewdrop falling on a lotus leaf. Some people are like the lotus leaf. The guru's teachings are like dewdrops. They fall on them and make them beautiful. Such people feel inspired by the guru's teachings, and may repeat them to others. They *want* to live according to those teachings—but they haven't assimilated them fully. Therefore, when a difficult situation arises, it's like

[32] Nitishatakam 67
[33] Thin pancake in South Indian cuisine made from a fermented batter of ground black lentils and rice

a gentle breeze blowing, and those teachings disappear—like the dewdrop falling off a leaf.

Once, I was talking with a friend while we were working. She said something that I disagreed with. I told her my perspective, which was different from hers. I could see she didn't like it. But she didn't reply or make any attempt to continue the discussion. Rather, she turned away and ignored me, carrying on with her work. I felt irritated. "How could she behave so rudely?" I felt like expressing my disapproval in a sarcastic comment, something like, "Oh, it's nice having a conversation with the wall!" Luckily, I held back. I carried on with my day and forgot about the incident.

That evening when I came to the hall for bhajans, I saw her from afar. My irritation from the morning resurfaced. On top of it, I felt irritated with myself for letting my mind be disturbed by such a small incident. I asked myself what advice Amma would give me to regain peace of mind.

Amma says, "The reason for most of the problems that occur in our life is our obstinacy—our unwillingness to accept things we don't like. We cannot change the world according to our whims and fancies. We should be able to adjust according to the situation we are up against. We must make ourselves capable of responding with discernment. We should learn to accept what is beyond our capacity to change. Prickly thorns surround a fragrant rose. It is futile to insist that the rose bush should have only roses and no thorns. Our mind will become mature only if we abandon such obstinacy. A mature mind remains content under any situation."

I sat in the bhajan hall on my meditation mat, thinking about Amma's words. I realized that though I had heard this teaching countless times, it had yet to really become a part of me. I had not yet translated it into my experience. And that's why I was still prone to getting irritated when I disliked someone's behavior. In that moment, all wisdom gathered from years of listening to Amma's teachings had vanished, like the dewdrop falling off a lotus leaf.

The third type of *śravaṇam* is like a raindrop falling into an oyster. It is said that if an oyster receives a drop of water at the time of the Swati constellation, that drop becomes a pearl. This represents the best kind of śravaṇam. In Amma's words, "We receive the teachings with our heart." In this kind of listening, we are open to the teachings of the guru, and contemplate them. We consciously try to incorporate that wisdom into our day-to-day experience. This way, the teachings go deep within our being. They become part of us, like how rain forms the precious pearl in the oyster.

If my *śravaṇam* had been truly like that, my irritation with my friend would have lasted only a few moments, if at all. I saw my failure. I had let myself get disturbed by something very insignificant. Also, I had lacked the expansiveness of mind to consider that there must be a reason for her behavior—that there are always two sides to a story, and her version of the conversation would probably be very different from mine.

It's not enough to simply hear the teachings of the guru and scriptures. It's also not enough to repeat them to others. We need to turn within, and really think about them. We need to try to implement them in our daily life, through our thoughts, words and actions. For that, we need to learn to watch ourselves—to watch our reactions to situations. This is not about making a grand commitment to become perfect overnight. Rather, it's about small, practical changes we can implement in our day. For instance, it can be helpful to keep track of what has been successful and what hasn't, on a daily basis.

Amma says, "Every night, a small businessman will evaluate his gains and losses, to make sure that he can carry on profitably. A big businessman need not do that daily because he has an established business. We are all beginners. We need to take account daily."

Through our introspection, contemplation and efforts to put the spiritual teachings into practice, we are slowly cultivating a precious pearl within us—a mind that is content, unperturbed and peaceful regardless of the external situation.

———

Patience in Our Interactions

One day, when I was speaking to my aunt on the phone, she told me about her neighbors. She wanted to talk about it because she was feeling upset seeing their situation. They have a two-year-old boy and a five-year-old girl. The parents both have good jobs. The grandmother also lives close by, and the kids regularly go and spend time with her. The children are delightful, and very lively. They often come to play in my aunt's house, as they live just next door. The family is very religious. Bright and inquisitive, the little girl often asks her mother questions related to spiritual and religious stories..

From the outside, it seems like an ideal family. But there is a problem. The father has an anger issue. He often loses his temper and shouts harshly at the kids for insignificant things. He doesn't listen to his wife when she protests, and he speaks to her in a loud, angry way.

Witnessing the effect this is having on the kids is painful to my aunt. She has noticed how the older child is becoming a little fearful and withdrawn. Not only does anger create a tense atmosphere in the family, it can also create behavior patterns that are passed down from generation to generation. Children grow up considering violent interactions as the norm. Alternatively, such children may suffer from anxiety, and later on find it difficult to trust people or develop close relationships.

The foundation of spirituality is the values that we adhere to in life. What is the use of offering our respect to representations of the divine in places of worship if we are unable to respect and be patient with others, especially our own family members?

141

Amma says, "We should lovingly cooperate and support each other for the common good of all, for the upliftment of the entire society. That is our true dharma, and it can take us to the ultimate goal of life, Self-realization. It should begin with the family."

Hearing this, some of us might think, "This is an important teaching, but it doesn't really apply to me. I'm not like the father in the story. Most of the time I'm loving and patient with my family members and other people around me." However, if we observe our thoughts and our words, we will usually find there is scope for improvement. Close and extended families are often hothouses of emotion, and can therefore provide good terrain for improving ourselves. And beyond that, let's reflect on how considerate and caring we are with the rest of society. In connection to this, Amma sometimes quotes lines from the bhajan Śakti Rupē:

> *ninne ninaccu koṇḍ-anyare drōhiccāl*
> *nin cinta entināṇu?*

> Divine Mother, what is the use of thinking of you if, while doing so, one hurts others?

> *kōvilil eṙe pradakṣiṇam ceytiṭṭā vātilil ninnu koṇḍu*
> *'māṙe'nnōti piccakkāre caviṭṭunna bhāvam vicitram allē?*

> Is it not strange if, after reverentially circumambulating the temple, one stands at the doorstep and kicks away the beggars?

"Kicking beggars" doesn't have to be taken literally. It could mean to speak insensitively to someone seeking our attention. It could be reacting with anger to someone who presses our buttons. It could be speaking harshly to someone who is coming at us with anger.

The Mahabharata talks of Kaushika, a renowned brahmin scholar. One day, as he was engaged in his practices, the excreta of a crane fell on his head. He looked up at the bird with such anger that the bird was reduced to a pile of ashes. The next day, Kaushika was in front of a house calling for alms. The lady of the house asked him to wait for a few minutes, and went inside to fetch food for him. By that time, her husband reached the house. He was hungry and tired. So, the lady served him food first, and gave alms to Kaushika only later.

Kaushika was angry and chastised her for making him wait. The woman was unperturbed, and coolly replied, "Don't think I'm a bird that can be scorched by your anger." Kaushika was dumbfounded. "How could she have known about the previous day's incident?" He realized that her intuitive power was due to her steadfastness in dharma.

She then tells Kaushika to meet a wise person named Dharmavyadha for a lesson on dharma. She emphasizes that this person is virtuous—not because he is a scholar or a brahmin but because he takes good care of his aged parents. She then explains to him that the sign of a pious person is not knowledge of the Vedas, but being free from anger and treating one's friends and family members with care and patience:

krodhaḥ śatruḥ śarīrastho manuṣyāṇāṁ dvijottama
yaḥ krodha-mohau tyajati taṁ devā brāhmaṇaṁ viduḥ

One's anger is one's enemy. The gods know that the
one who knows his true nature is one who has cast off
anger and passion.[34]

---

[34] Mahabharata 3.197.31

This is a conversation between a seemingly ordinary housewife and a brahmin scholar. Yet who is giving the spiritual advice? The housewife. Not the scholar. Kaushika may have studied the Vedas extensively, but the woman's life is rooted in dharma. Her words reflect qualities such as patience, an attitude of service and forgiveness. Such qualities are the real foundation of spirituality.

Going to temples, chanting spiritual texts, meditating—these are all important. However, they are not the real measures of our spiritual progress. That is reflected through our relationships—with our family, our friends, and with everyone else with whom we interact.

Listening with the Heart

Amma says, "We have no practice listening carefully to others. Therefore, most of us are not good listeners; we are only speakers. If we are able to become good listeners, many problems in life will be solved. In order to prevent discussions from becoming arguments, instead of focusing on establishing your own point of view, try to listen and understand the view of the other person."

We often do not listen to each other because we are absorbed in our own world. Even amongst family members, we can see a similar pattern. It is like two simultaneous monologues under the disguise of a dialogue.

One person says, "I am feeling a little feverish."

The other says, "Oh really? I had a terrible fever a few weeks ago. It went on for several days. I felt terrible"

The first one says, "Yes, I have to see a doctor tomorrow."

The second person says, "Doctor? Oh, I didn't go to the doctor. I took paracetamol and my mother's lemon and honey tea. But now I kind of wish I had gone to see the doctor because it might not have dragged on for so many days. And now I still have the remnants of a cough that developed later on." This kind of dialog may sound like a familiar scenario for most of us. We may not always realize how little we really listen to others.

Once, a friend behaved in a way that I thought was incorrect. I felt strongly about it and wanted to tell her. I found her and started telling her that she had behaved unfairly. Immediately, she became defensive, and the conversation quickly became an argument. After some time, it didn't look like we were going to agree on anything.

She wasn't listening to my perspective, and I didn't want to waste any more time and energy arguing. I was about to leave. She must have realized that because suddenly her tone changed. Her eyes filled with tears, and she said, "I just really need you to listen to me right now. I need to be heard and understood. Please."

Hearing those words, I stopped. For the first time, I became truly quiet and actually listened to what she had to say. She explained her side, and it became clear to me why she had acted the way she had. Her behavior was stemming from her inner suffering. I understood that underlying her indiscriminate action was a craving for love. Having been able to express herself, feeling heard and understood, she calmed down. I then gently explained why I felt her action had been inappropriate. She heard and understood, and the conversation ended in a constructive way, on a positive note.

Many of us would agree that the first part of our interaction is a scenario that is all too common in family life. We disagree on something or disapprove of the behavior of one of our family members. We then express our disapproval abruptly, before sincerely trying to understand the reason behind that person's words or actions. Having been criticized, the other person typically becomes defensive. We all do this. If someone criticizes our words or actions—at the slightest prick to our ego—we react. We embark on a series of justifications and arguments to prove that we are right, that we are blameless, and that the other person is in the wrong.

Such disagreements could easily be avoided, if we have the patience to listen to each other. If we want healthy relationships, we need the humility and maturity to put aside our defensive attitude and listen with our heart.

In this incident, I should not have started the conversation with, "What you did was wrong." If I had instead approached her by saying, "I didn't understand your action that day. Could you tell me what happened? I'd like to hear your version," then the argument could have been avoided altogether.

The situation was saved not by my maturity but by the other person being open about how she felt. Her words were a wake-up call for me—a reminder to be patient and to listen. But most of the time the other person doesn't tell us clearly that they need us to listen and to understand. They also get angry. So, it's essential that we remember to listen. We need to try to understand the point of view of the other person and to make them feel heard.

In the Vana Parva, one of the books of the Mahabharata, we see the equivalent of a "family argument." It was the 13th month of exile of the Pandavas. The conversation has a lot of depth, but here I'll focus on only one aspect of it. It's about a man and wife who listened to each other. They understood each other's imperfections and yet still had the patience to listen to each other. Draupadi appealed to Yudhishthira to wreak vengeance on the Kauravas. Yudhishthira listened to her and said, "Draupadi, we have listened attentively to your words."

He then elaborated on the importance of forgiveness and patience. Yudhishthira told Draupadi that her view was not in line with higher dharma. In reply, Draupadi had the clarity and honesty to explain that her words arose from her frustration at their situation.

She said, "In the midst of my overwhelming sorrow, Yudhishthira, please realize that my words stem from a state of sheer distress and anguish. And I must warn you, this is not the end of it; there will be a recurrence of my lamentations in the future. You can expect that, deeply immersed in my sorrows, I will once again express my grief."

The family discussion went on like this. Even when their views differed, the spouses spoke with mutual respect. They gave each other the time to express their thoughts and feelings. We can learn a lot from this example.

Amma says, "Real listening happens only when you listen with your heart, with love. Learn to respect each other's feelings. Learn to listen to each other's problems with love and concern."

A couple of years after I joined the ashram, I was facing a challenge. I felt sad but didn't know who to turn to. One day, when I was sitting a few people away from Amma, she looked at me and motioned for me to come close. So, I went near and whispered into her ear, in English, one sentence that summarized my mental state. Amma looked into my eyes, and also in English said, "I understand."

That was enough—just to feel understood. In that very second, I felt like I had put down a huge burden I had been carrying around. No one in the world listens to others as much as Amma does. She has listened to countless people of all ages, backgrounds, cultures and walks of life. We get so much solace from talking to Amma because she is fully present. Amma listens completely from her heart

Everyone longs to be understood. When we listen to someone, we are offering them a gift, the gift of our attention, of our time. At the same time, when we learn to listen, we also benefit. Our mind becomes more expansive. We become enriched by understanding perspectives that are different from ours. We learn about how human beings work, how our minds function. We naturally learn to be more tolerant and patient.

Language of the Heart

From his hiding place on the branch of the shimshapa tree, Hanuman wondered what to do. Now that he had finally found the gentle Sita, he was at a loss as to how to approach her. What if she suspected him to be sent by her abductor, Ravana, to trick her into giving in to him? At the same time, Hanuman knew he had to talk to her to bring her the news of her beloved Rama. Suddenly, he had an ingenious idea. Being careful to remain hidden in the foliage he crept along the branch, to come closer to Sita.

Overwhelmed with grief, Sita stood beneath the ashoka tree, staring into the darkness. Her large eyes were sad and bewildered. She, who had never known sorrow, couldn't conceive of the tragedy that had befallen her. Since Ravana had captured her, every moment had been a nightmare.

Suddenly, out of the sky, there was a little voice. It sounded as though it was speaking to itself. "There was once a king named Dasharatha. His strength and valor were renowned in the three worlds. He had four sons. The eldest was Rama, and the king loved him more than life itself."

Those words went straight to Sita's heart. A tide of hope swept over her. A light of wonder and faith danced in her big eyes as she listened to those life-giving words.

Amma says, "Through words, we can travel both to our inner world and to the external world. Words hold the way to inner freedom—the way to goodness, and the way to love. In all our words, there is a potent seed. We need inner strength for our words to become like a tree that gives shade, coolness and fruits to others. Let's not underestimate the power of kind words."

Once I was talking to a long-term devotee of Amma's who lives in Uttarakhand. She runs an NGO dedicated to fighting violence against women and children. Recently, a woman had called her NGO's helpline.

This woman was from the Philippines. She had met her Indian husband there. After the birth of their first child, they settled in Haryana—close to her husband's family. They had two more children. Then, in 2020, the woman's husband died of COVID. She now lived with her in-laws. Her husband's brother was sexually abusing her, and wanted to force her to marry him. He had hidden her passport and other important documents, so there was no escape. The rest of the family kept quiet. The woman knew very little Hindi and very little English. She was extremely isolated.

Desperate, and seeing no way out of the horrible situation, the woman decided to take her own life, along with those of her three small children. But before she did so, she saw the NGO's helpline number on TV and decided to call. It was her very last attempt—her last hope. After hearing her story, the devotee told her that they would rescue her, but that it would take a few days because she was in another state, and they had to complete some paperwork with the police first.

The thought of having to stay in her situation any longer was too much for the woman. She said, "Every moment is a nightmare. I don't think I can survive a day longer. I can't! It's better we all just die. At least none of us will be left in this hell."

Nothing the devotee said seemed to calm the woman down and turn her away from the idea of suicide. The devotee then tried another strategy. Amazingly, she knew a little Filipino. She tried speaking to the poor lady in whatever broken Filipino she could remember: "My dear, don't worry. Be assured we are coming for you, as fast as we can. We will definitely rescue you and your children. Don't lose hope. Just wait for us. We are coming."

Those loving words in the lady's mother tongue had a magical effect. She calmed down and agreed to wait. Those words gave her the strength to persevere. A few days later, she was rescued, and she and her children were returned to her family in the Philippines.

When the devotee lovingly spoke to the lady in her mother tongue, the words went straight to her heart. They brought a ray of hope into the heavy darkness that surrounded her.

It's not that we need to learn all languages to be able to have heart-to-heart communication with everyone. Fortunately, the devotee did know some Filipino, but more than the language, it was the kindness and thoughtfulness behind those words that had such a soothing effect on the woman. There is one language that is universal, bridging all differences of culture and nationality. That is Amma's language—the language that has endeared her to millions across the globe. It is the language of love.

Swami Amritaswarupananda Puri, Amma's most senior disciple, once said, "Amma is able to establish perfect communication with people of all nations, languages and cultures because her real language is not Malayalam but a universal one—the language of love. Amma is able to communicate through the language of love because she understands people's hearts—their deep-seated sorrows, their hidden pains. Through her compassionate presence and personal bond with millions of people across the globe—people from all walks of life, people who speak various languages and come from various cultural backgrounds—Amma proves that love can indeed be a universal language."

Amma says, "We are interested in learning more and more languages, which are the means to communicate with people from other parts of the country and the world. But we've completely forgotten the language of love and compassion—the language of the heart—which more than anything else, helps us to understand one another."

Hanuman's words brought hope to Sita's heart. The devotee's words brought solace and courage to the woman in that desperate situation. There is a Sanskrit saying that goes:

priya-vākya-pradānena sarve tuṣyanti jantavaḥ
tasmāt-tad-eva vaktavyaṁ vacane kā daridratā

Kind and loving words make all beings happy;
so, we should speak such words. Why should
there be scarcity of kind words in one's speech?

———⌣⌣⌣———

9

We are Part of a Whole

Amma says, "No one is an isolated island. We are all joined to one another like the links of a chain." Spirituality isn't about setting ourselves apart from the rest of society. It is about coming out of our narrow world that revolves around "I" to realize we are connected to something much bigger. That shift in mindset spontaneously translates into a genuine desire for the well-being of others and actions that benefit the whole.

Real Renunciation

After finishing school, I came to India to stay in the ashram for a year. I flew into Trivandrum and took the public bus from the airport. When I got onto the bus in Karunagappally for the last leg of the journey, two brahmacharinis (female monastics) from the ashram were on the same bus. I was only 17 at the time—a young spiritual aspirant bubbling with enthusiasm—so I was delighted to be able to sit next to them.

One of those brahmacharinis was very skinny. Sitting in the bus, from the corner of my eye I looked at her thin arms, and told my teenage mind emphatically: "Look and remember this! Remember this as your ideal when engaged in fasting, burning up your attachment to the body in the fire of renunciation!"

Looking back, I can only laugh at my narrow concept of renunciation at that time. First of all, that brahmacharini is just naturally skinny. But still I imagined the spiritual path to be about vows, strict discipline and self-inflicted bodily austerities. With such an image in mind, no wonder people get a little scared at the very mention of the word renunciation.

Let us look at what it really represents. The Kaivalya Upanishad says: *na karmaṇā na prajayā dhanena tyāgenaike amṛtatvamānaśuḥ.*[35] This is also the motto of Amma's ashram. It means, "Immortality is not attained through actions, nor through progeny or wealth. Rather, it is only obtained through renunciation."

---

[35] Kaivalya Upanishad, verse 3

The word I've translated as "renunciation"—*tyāga*—comes from the root word *tyaj*, which means "destruction," "leaving," "abandoning." We always desire to gain, to get more and more. It is therefore natural that at the very mention of "giving up" or "renouncing" something, we become tense. The reason why we may feel uneasy hearing the words of the Upanishad about renunciation is because we don't have a real understanding of what immortality is. In reality, it is moksha—liberation. And Adi Shankaracharya[36] tells us that liberation is *atyāntika duḥkha nivṛtti*—the ultimate cessation of suffering. Phrased like that, renunciation sounds more appealing.

For all our life, we have all been doing the same thing. Every day, we have the same agenda: looking for happiness. If we are honest, most of us will probably agree that so far, we haven't been entirely successful in our search. Broadly, we all search for happiness in the same things: external comfort, love and approval from people around us, acceptance and respect from the broader community. The moments of dissatisfaction that we experience are an indication that we are not searching for happiness in the right place. Still, rather than learning from this and trying to seek elsewhere, we usually continue searching in the same way.

Amma says, "If our child is sick, we will take many days off from work to nurse our child back to health. We are ready to go to court any number of times to gain a single cent of land. We might forgo sleep to work overtime in order to make more money. We cannot call any of these an act of renunciation. Only actions done without the attitude of 'I' and 'mine,' for the welfare of the world and as an offering to God, can be called

---

[36] Renowned exponent of Advaita Vedanta. His commentaries continue to serve as the basis of the Advaita interpretation of the Vedas, making him one of the most influential figures in the history of Indian philosophy.

renunciation. Such self-sacrificing acts open the doors to the world of the Self."

Lord Krishna, Jesus, Amma—those enlightened gurus who know the secret to contentment—tell us that happiness lies in letting go of our self-centeredness and pettiness. While fasting and reducing possessions etc., all play a role, self-centeredness and pettiness are the real things that we should try to renounce. This is because in reality, they are the root of our suffering.

Imagine a person is complaining about the foul smell in a room full of trash. Someone tells him, "You need to get rid of that waste. Then the stink will go." But our person is uneasy at the idea of having to get rid of anything. He therefore sticks his fingers in his ears and pretends he cannot hear. In a way, we are similar to this person. We complain about being unhappy. And when the great masters tell us to let go of what is making us suffer—all the "trash" we keep in our mind—we pretend not to hear.

Once we understand the true source of happiness, we won't see renunciation as anything unpleasant. It will stop appearing like a hardship. It will become clear to us that it is the way to end our suffering. Once we realize that it is the trash piled up in our room that is causing the unbearable stink, we will naturally want to get rid of the trash.

A practical tool to start renouncing our negativities is to help others—to try to be sensitive to their suffering. Amma always says, "Never waste an opportunity to offer a helping hand to someone in need."

A friend of my mother who lives in the UK takes care of her elderly mother, and also gives a lot of her time and energy to her adult children, one of whom suffers from mental-health problems. The other child has children of her own and relies on my mother's friend for help with childcare. She is a very kind, giving person, and her life revolves around taking care of the needs of others.

At one point, she confided in my mother that she felt tired, both physically and mentally. She realized that she needed a break. She arranged for some people to help her mother when she'd be gone and booked a seaside room for a few days. It was going to be like a retreat. The plan was to simply enjoy the solitude without having to worry about anyone else for a few days. She was really looking forward to a time of recharging, spending time alone in nature.

The next time my mother spoke to her friend on the phone, she asked about her upcoming trip. My mother's friend replied, "Well, put it this way, the nature of the trip has changed a little."

"Oh, but you were so excited about it," replied my mother. "What happened?"

My mother's friend explained: "An old friend of mine called recently. She struggles with her mental health and is quite depressed at the moment, poor thing. When I told her about my trip, she asked if she could come along too. And you know, I just couldn't say no. She's going through a hard time, and I know it means a lot to her."

This is a true example of *tyāga*, of renunciation. My mother's friend prioritized the needs of someone else—someone who wasn't even directly related to her—before her own. She was ready to sacrifice her highly anticipated alone time for the sake of someone else's happiness.

Does this mean that fasting, vows, and observing a spiritual discipline are not needed? No. Such practices can be valuable tools, because they make us become more aware of how our mind works and help us strengthen our will-power. Only through real effort and determination can we succeed in uprooting our selfish tendencies. A mind devoid of selfishness is a blessing for the world. At the same time, we needn't become discouraged thinking such complete renunciation is out of our reach. Any small attempt to step beyond our selfishness is also a blessing.

In the ashram on a Tuesday, after meditation, Amma said, "Renunciation is the patience and love we show to others. It may be to have the patience to listen to the suffering of someone we don't know. It may be to help someone up from a fall. It may be to share our food with someone who is hungry. All these are forms of renunciation, especially when it's people we don't know. It is leaving the attitude of 'I' and 'mine' to come to the attitude that all are children of the supreme. That is renunciation—arising and awakening to that attitude."

Light in the Dark

It was a pitch-dark night in Mathura.[37] Not even a glimmer of moonlight. Heavy rains poured down and winds threatened to destroy everything in the way. Many guards stood outside the heavy door to the dungeon. Inside the dungeon, it was dark and cheerless. Devaki and Vasudeva were from royal families, but they had no bed. They lay on the cold, stone floor. Heavy chains bound Devaki to a pillar. Vasudeva was chained to another pillar, several feet away. They were weighed down by sorrow, the grief from having lost every one of their newborn children to Kamsa.[38]

It was in that situation of intense hardship that Lord Krishna was born. It was in that intense darkness that the Lord came as a tiny baby shining like a brilliant sun of hope and goodness: *svarociṣā virocayantam sūtikāgṛham*[39]—"The little one's effulgence illuminated the entire room."

In our life, we can try to remember that our times of difficulty can also be periods of transformation. It sometimes seems like the world is in quite a dark period, and life can feel like being in a long, dark tunnel with no end in sight. But we need to remember and see that difficulties and calamities also have a way of bringing out the best in humanity.

Amma says, "When difficult situations arise, we should try to use them to gather mental strength so that we can grow, rise

---

[37] Birthplace of Lord Krishna
[38] The couple were imprisoned by Devaki's brother Kamsa, after he heard the prediction that he would be killed by Devaki's eighth child.
[39] Srimad Bhagavatam 10.3.12

up, and move to action. We have been given this human birth in order to face challenges and overcome them, not to run away from them. A ship at sea has to weather storms, rough seas and may even encounter whales or sharks, while the ship anchored in the harbor doesn't face any such challenges. However, who would make a ship just to moor it in the harbor? When obstacles appear in life, we need to kindle our inner strength and spread the fragrance of selflessness and love. We should be able to lift up others who are drowning in grief."

During the COVID pandemic, so many healthcare workers went out of their way to try to provide not only medical care but also emotional support and solace. But such sparks of selflessness were not limited to health workers. People from all walks of life stepped forward to volunteer in one way or another. At the beginning of the pandemic, my elderly parents told me that people in their neighborhood had organized a help network for those more vulnerable—senior citizens and the sick. Through that, help was offered to my parents without them even having to ask for it. For example, volunteers would take care of their grocery shopping. These were people they had never met before.

In India, AYUDH, the youth wing of the Mata Amritanandamayi Math, assisted people during the crisis in all sorts of ways. Hundreds of volunteers ran medical helplines, locating hospital beds and organizing supplies.

One AYUDH member from Delhi, shared with me a heart-wrenching story. "I cannot forget that one instance when I received a call from a patient's son and he said, 'I need an oxygen cylinder. I have already lost my mother and brother to COVID, and now my father is also infected and in a very serious condition. I have been running all day and night looking for oxygen but have not been able to find any. I don't even have time to cry.'

"After hearing this, I could not stop my tears. We tried from dawn to dusk, and finally, in the late evening, we got an oxygen cylinder. The man was so relieved and happy. He thanked us profusely and said, 'You've saved my father's life.'"

Another area where the spirit of *vasudhaiva kuṭumbakam* (the world is one family) proved to be a lifesaver for many, was food. Numerous food-help networks formed across India. Many people would even get up extra early to cook before going to work at the office or elsewhere, providing home-cooked meals to patients and healthcare workers.

There were countless such incidents—incidents of people going out of their way to offer a helping hand to strangers. The goodness of humanity shines through such incidents. Everywhere in the world, we saw people stepping up and helping others. This is a light of hope in the darkness—like the radiance of baby Krishna that shone through the heavy darkness hanging over the jail in Mathura. Amma always tells us that the birth of the divine is to happen within our heart. That birth takes place when our heart fills with goodness and compassion.

Amma says, "The fragrance of a flower travels only in the direction of the wind. However, the fragrance of goodness travels equally in all directions. We may be unable to help everyone in this world. But if we are able to express our compassion to a few people around us, they will pass it on, and very soon it will spread all around."

Rather than fretting over the grim state of things, we can open our eyes and look around. There will always be some kind of opportunity for us to make our little contribution—an opportunity for little gestures of compassion. We can try to think beyond our self-centered, narrow world and find ways to reach out to those who could do with a helping hand. As Amma says, together, we can spread the light of compassion, chasing away the darkness.

Be the Change

One day, a devotee from Europe called me and spoke about her difficult situation. Her daughter, a mother of three, had lost her job and had moved back home. She had found a new part-time job but couldn't afford a place of her own. This had been going on for almost two years, and it was far from a harmonious situation. There were often arguments between the devotee and her daughter. Now, with the COVID lockdown, they were all stuck together in the small house! Worse yet, following an argument, the daughter completely stopped talking to her parents. The devotee was at her wits end: "I've lost all peace of mind. I've even been looking into renting a room somewhere. That way at least *I* could move out of this miserable situation."

I asked her, "Can't someone help you? Couldn't you go all together to see a family therapist to try to improve the communication between you? Don't such therapists or mediators exist over there?"

She replied, "Yes, yes, they do exist. That's my daughter's job. She is a family therapist."

What could I say to that? I didn't have any other solutions to offer. Still, she seemed happy just to have been able to talk to someone about her situation.

The next week, the devotee called me again. She said, "One morning, I prayed to Amma about our situation at home. Just a little later, I came across this quote of Amma: "Every action we perform—consciously or unconsciously, alone or as a group—reflects in every corner of the universe. Things won't work if we wait for others to change. Even if they do not change, we should be willing to change. We should see what we can do."

She told me, "These words felt like an answer to my prayer. I was reminded that instead of trying to change my daughter, I should change my attitude. Before going to work, my daughter usually leaves a note for me regarding the kids' schedule. Yesterday, instead of simply taking it quietly, I held it up and asked my daughter lovingly, 'Is this note for me?'

"She looked quite taken aback. She hadn't expected I'd talk to her, seeing as it had been several months since she had spoken to me. She stammered, 'Um, yes, it is.' The next day, before setting off for work, my daughter spoke to me. She said, 'Mum, I'll only be back late today. Would you put a portion of the evening meal in the oven to stay warm for when I come back?'

"I said, 'Of course.' This was such a surprise. It was the first time that my daughter had looked at my face and spoken to me in months!"

The devotee went on to tell me how through this incident, she had seen the truth of Amma's words. A small shift in her own attitude and behavior had produced a visible effect on the whole situation.

In difficult situations at home or at work, a single person's positive attitude can diffuse a lot of tension. One person's good intentions can temper many negative dynamics.

In Ayodhya, the terrible news of Rama's exile had cast a shadow of gloom over the palace. The entire royal family was shattered. Only Rama stayed composed in the midst of his ordeal. His father, King Dasharatha, was so beside himself with grief that he kept losing his senses. Queen Kausalya was in a similar state and was weeping piteously. Seeing Kausalya's grief, Lakshmana was all the more angry towards their father, Dasharatha.

Rama, Sita and Lakshmana were about to depart. The whole atmosphere was heavy with grief and resentment. But one person maintained a courageous and noble attitude. That was Sumitra, Dasharatha's third queen. The situation was just as heart-wrenching for her; she would be separated from her son, Lakshmana, for 14 years. Still, she spoke the perfect words to guide Lakshmana on his journey:

> *rāmam daśaratham viddhi mām viddhi janaka ātmajām*
> *ayodhyām aṭavīm viddhi gacca tāta yathā sukham*

> Consider Rama as your father, Sita as your mother, and the forest as Ayodhya, and go in peace, my son.[40]

These words uplifted the whole atmosphere, shifting everyone's focus from what they could not control to what they could—their attitudes. Sumitra's words were like a ray of light, dissipating the darkness of anger, resentment and sorrow. Her loving words transformed a family tragedy into a moment to embrace dharma.

Sumitra didn't wait for the other's attitudes to shift. She had the courage and nobility to be that positive change herself.

This situation in the Ramayana may seem distant from our modern-day world. We are not as compassionate, patient and established in dharma as Lord Rama or Sumitra. That is okay. However, if we observe closely, we will find that often, a small adjustment in our attitude can have a big impact in a difficult situation.

Amma says, "Don't try to change the world or other people before you are able to change yourself. If you try to change

---

[40] Ramayana 2.40.9

others without changing your own attitude, it will not have any effect. Change yourself; then the world around you will also change."

Pray for the Deceased

Ravana, the demon king of Lanka, had captured Sita and taken her away. A distraught Rama and Lakshmana were wandering in search of any sign of her whereabouts. They came to a clearing in the forest, and there they saw Jatayu, their bird friend, lying on the ground. Rama rushed forward and took the big bird in his arms. Jatayu was dying, and could barely speak. He had somehow hung on to life just so he could see Rama before breathing his last. He spoke in a whisper, "Rama, it is Ravana who has taken away Sita. He has taken her far away from here. He went towards the south, child—towards the south."

The old bird's eyes then closed in exhaustion. Opening them once more, he said, "Hold me in your arms, Rama. My eyes have lost their vision, and I am going now. O Rama! It is my fortune to die in your lap." Then life ebbed away from Jatayu. He closed his eyes a final time and passed away peacefully in Rama's arms.

Rama's eyes filled with tears. He whispered, "Only a father would offer his life like this for the sake of his child.[41] Collect some wood, Lakshmana, let us cremate him with honor."

With the great bird's body in his arms, Rama walked slowly towards the Godavari River. Lakshmana made a bed of *darbha*[42] grass on the ground. Rama gently laid the body on it. Lakshmana covered the corpse with dry branches and twigs.

Rama said, "O Father, king of birds, may you reach the heaven meant for great ascetics. Virtuous Jatayu, may your journey be blessed!"

---

[41] Jatayu had tried to attack Ravana as he carried Sita away.
[42] A type of grass traditionally used in rituals

Rama rubbed two twigs together and lit the pyre. He offered his salutation to the departed soul. He offered the ceremonial *piṇḍā*,[43] and recited the verses for *śrāddha*.[44] The brothers then bathed in the waters of the Godavari. Standing in the river, they offered water oblations for Jatayu. The noble bird rose towards the realm of the most exalted sages.

Offering prayers and performing rites after the death of a near and dear one is an important way of expressing our gratitude and love. It also creates a conducive atmosphere for the soul of the departed to continue its journey. Sanatana Dharma says that the soul travels from body to body in a continuous cycle of births and deaths, from which we are freed only upon spiritual liberation. But even if we feel unsure regarding what happens after death, praying for the well-being and peace of the departed can have a beneficial and soothing effect on the one offering those prayers. It is also freeing for us, as it helps bring a sense of both closure and connection. Not that it will end our grief; grief takes time. But rather than our being swallowed up in our sense of loss, prayer enables us to have a brighter, more constructive focus.

Regarding the rites performed for the sake of the deceased, Amma says, "Our focus is always on what we can get, never on what we can give. We grow up because our parents and near ones gave to us. In truth, that debt cannot be repaid. Through this ritual, we are showing our respect and gratitude towards our departed ancestors. Our gratitude shouldn't remain only at a verbal level. It should manifest as action. By partaking in this ritual, we are performing action—spending some time for others, spending some money for them, and chanting mantras. Through this, we create positive vibrations and get purified."

---

[43] Ceremonial offering of food to the deceased.
[44] Ceremony in honor of and for the benefit of deceased relatives.

Partaking in traditional rites may not always be possible. Even so, there is a lot of value in merely lighting a lamp and spending some time praying for our departed loved one's well-being. We will benefit, and Amma assures us that those positive vibrations definitely reach those for whom they are intended.

Amma always tells us that death is not a complete annihilation. Rather, it is like putting a period at the end of a sentence. After a pause, life continues, just like a new sentence does. Death is a passage—a step on a journey. Trying to give our near and dear ones a positive send-off through prayer will facilitate their passage.

Once, a friend told me about a young man who had been severely injured in an accident. The doctors said he only had a few days to live. He had slipped into a coma and showed no signs of life other than his labored breathing. His mother, who had been in a state of shock, slowly and sadly realized that her son would never wake up. It was unbearable to see her son suffering like that. She wanted him to be released from his agony. But she felt something was holding him back, hindering him from leaving his body. So, the grief-stricken mother gently whispered into her son's ear, "It's okay darling, you can go. You are in too much pain in this body. It's okay my child, you can go." On some level, it was his mother's sorrow and her inability to accept his departure that were holding him back. In a way, that soul was as if waiting for his mother to give him permission to go. Because only a few hours after she whispered those words in his ear, he passed, peacefully.

A dying person may be distressed at causing grief for loved ones. On such occasions, they may leave only when they have been given "permission" like this young boy was given by his mother. We can imagine it is similar after death. Having left the body, the soul can remain reluctant to leave this realm. Our prayers provide the love and acceptance they need to move forward, instead of remaining bound by the ties of our sorrow.

Prayer is a powerful tool. When we pray, we develop trust in a higher force, a divinity that is within us, that we connect to when we pray. Words are potent. If insults and derogatory words can pull us down, then loving words, words expressing gratitude, words wishing well, can certainly uplift us. Through prayer, we tap into our inner strength and goodness. Along with prayer, we can also do good deeds in memory of the departed soul, like giving money to charity.

Amma says, "Your prayers will never be wasted; you should gain strength thinking of that." We can pray wholeheartedly for our loved ones, but also for all departed souls: *lokāḥ samastāḥ sukhino bhavantu*—"May all beings in all the worlds be happy."

The World is One Family

I was always fascinated by India, years before setting foot here. My mother had visited India in her youth, and I would regularly ask her about it. My parents gave me a big book of photos of India, and I would go through its pages eagerly. My first experience of India, before my actual visit, was a small pocket of India I encountered in the town where I attended school in France.

I must have been 15 at the time. It was a Tamil family's small apartment—a mini bubble of Indian culture within a French city. I was fascinated! There were images of various gods on the walls, and I still remember the delicious aromas coming from the kitchen.

They had a little boy, who must have been under two years old. And the mother kept telling him, "Akka, akka." At that time, I had no idea what that word meant. I thought maybe it was a pet name for him. She kept on repeating, "Akka, akka." She didn't speak English and knew only a little French, and of course at that time I had no idea of Malayalam, let alone Tamil. Yet we somehow managed to communicate.

It was only a year later, when I actually came to India that I understood that akka meant "elder sister." I realized that this lady, who had never met me before, was teaching her son to see me—a teenager from a different culture, speaking a different language—as an elder sister. This revelation left a deep impression on me. What a rich culture India has—one that considers even complete strangers and foreigners as part of one's extended family. That idea is expressed in the Vedic concept *vasudhaiva kuṭumbakam*—"The world is a family." It is expressed in the Maha Upanishad:

> *ayam nijaḥ paro veti gaṇanā laghu-cetasām*
> *udāracaritānāṁ tu vasudhaiva kuṭumbakam*

Only the narrow-minded think, "This is mine, that is his." The wise, on the other hand, consider the entire world to be a family.[45]

Lord Krishna also expresses the same idea in the Bhagavad Gita when he says, *mayi sarvam idaṁ protaṁ sūtre maṇi-gaṇā iva*— "Everything rests in me, like beads strung on a thread."[46]

In the Maha Upanishad, the context of this verse is a discussion on the state of spiritual liberation. Ultimately, this concept comes from the most expansive vision—the state of supreme knowledge in which everything is perceived as one's own Self. That is Amma's vision. Amma's vision is all-encompassing, seeing everything as part of her Self. This is translated into her actions. She is the mother for whom the whole world is one family. That vision of hers is expressed through her tireless giving of herself every minute in the service of others, breaking the boundaries of culture, religion, gender and nationality. For Amma, it's a state of being. For us, *vasudhaiva kuṭumbakam* is an outlook that we can strive to put into practice. If we don't put in effort to make it come to life in our day-to-day activities, it will remain merely a lofty principle—words in a book gathering dust on a shelf.

We can see from this Vedic ethos that Sanatana Dharma's vision is deeply inclusive. This is reflected today in the everyday customs such as addressing even strangers as "acchan" (father),

---

[45] Maha Upanishad 6.71
[46] Bhagavad Gita 7.7

"amma" (mother), "chechi" (sister),[47] and the tradition of treating the guest like a god. These are not mere mechanical customs to be implemented through words and gestures. Rather, they are attitudes to awaken in our heart. That is where the expansive vision of *vasudhaiva kuṭumbakam*—the world as one family—needs to be established.

This is needed because the reality is that our minds are often narrow; frequently, our default position is to be judgmental. If we watch our mind carefully, we can see this. There is a relentless nagging voice, "Oh, she is wearing that kind of shoe, so she must be like this," "He is overweight; he is probably lazy," "She always wears flashy colors. She must want attention." These types of judgements stem from our limited perspectives, and generally do not represent the entirety of a situation. We need to recognise our preconceived notions and try to be more open when it comes to others. We will be the first to benefit. Our assumptions are put into our head by others. If we develop the capacity to think for ourselves and sincerely try to understand others, we will be able to respect them more genuinely.

As the Upanishad suggests, that which limits our perspective is our sense of "mine." If we can expand this sense of "mine" and make it all-encompassing, we will find our outlook entirely transformed. Sanatana Dharma tells us that the same divine truth is the essence within all of us. Therefore, we can try to see others not as separate from us, but as our own. When someone tells us, "I feel proud of you," it makes us feel so happy. Why? Because it comes from an inclusive vision. Someone has indirectly told us, "You are in my camp, you are one of my people." If we try to view all people as our own, we will spontaneously feel love and compassion.

---

[47] These terms are in Malayalam, but almost all other Indian languages have similar practices.

In a letter to a man who was distraught over the death of his young son from polio, Einstein wrote, "A human being is a part of the whole called by us universe, a part limited in time and space. He experiences himself, his thoughts and feelings as something separated from the rest, a kind of optical delusion of his consciousness. This delusion is a kind of prison for us, restricting us to our personal desires and to affection for a few persons nearest to us. Our task must be to free ourselves from this prison by widening our circle of compassion to embrace all living creatures and the whole of nature in its beauty."

We can try to cultivate such an expansive vision, viewing everyone as part of "our camp," of "our people." Because we are all *amṛtasya putrāḥ*—children of the divine.[48]

---

[48] Svetasvatara Upanishad

10

Navigating Life

The scriptures say, *mana eva manuṣyāṇāṁ kāraṇaṁ bandha-mokṣayoḥ*—"For human beings, the mind is the cause for both bondage and liberation."[49] If we understand the workings of the mind and use that very mind to understand the nature of the world and its impermanence, we will be able to go through life without becoming too emotionally disturbed. Beyond that, we will be able to grow through every situation we encounter and even appreciate the journey and experiences along the way.

---

[49] Brahmabindu Upanishad, verse 2

Understand the Nature of the World

Once someone left an unripe jackfruit from the garden on the kitchen's deliveries table. I decided to cook it because I know it makes a nice thoran.[50] I had cooked idichakka (tender jackfruit) before, but this was the first time I was going to prepare a full-size jackfruit. Preparing the jackfruit entails removing the fruit's flesh from its thick skin, removing the seeds and cleaning it. In my enthusiasm, I thought I'd have a go at it. But no one else was in the kitchen, and therefore there was no one I could approach for instructions.

Patience is not my strength, so I didn't want to waste my time looking for someone to ask. I took the biggest knife I could find and placed the jackfruit—which weighed about five kilograms—on the table. I stuck the knife into it and kept rotating the fruit on the table in an attempt to cut it into two. But then, I tried to pull out the knife. I pulled very hard, and it finally came out, but it was coated with sap. Sap was on the blade, the handle and even on my hands. Still, I was not going to stop. I inserted the knife again and continued cutting the fruit down into more manageable pieces. Meanwhile, the oozing sap continued to spread.

I wanted to wipe my hand to get a better grip on the knife, but what could I wipe it with? I suddenly noticed that my phone was dangerously close to the messy sticky area on the table. I took it with my fingertips, but could barely put it down again,

---

[50] Traditional Kerala dish of vegetable with coconut

as the phone case was sticking to them. So, the sticky sap was on the phone too.

I turned on the tap to try to wash my hands—the tap became all sticky. And water didn't seem to do anything to remove the sap. I tried using soap, lathering it well, but it wasn't much help. Finally, I remembered seeing people use oil for this. I thought I'd give it a try. Sure enough, after rubbing my hands with oil, the sticky substance started to come off. I proceeded to rub the knife, table and my phone case with oil. After oil, I used soap and water. Finally, I was able to get everything clean.

I had learned my lesson. Before resuming cutting the jackfruit, I spread out some newspaper and placed the jackfruit on top. I applied oil once more to my hands and the knife. After that, the process went smoothly. In the end, everyone enjoyed the thoran.

This is the kind of thing that happens when a foreigner comes across a jackfruit! I subsequently found out that the sap of jackfruits is sometimes used as an adhesive. Beyond providing entertainment, this incident taught me an important lesson. I remembered something Amma had said a few days before: "Spirituality is not about living away from the world. It's about living in the world while understanding its nature. Just as armor protects the soldier, spiritual knowledge protects us from the difficulties of life."

Reflecting on Amma's words, I thought, "If living in the world is compared to preparing a jackfruit, spirituality is the oil we need to apply to our fingers!" Without the protective oil of spiritual knowledge, the sap of life makes a sticky mess. What is this spiritual knowledge? It is understanding the nature of the world—the nature of people and objects around us.

Amma says, "We must become capable of responding with discernment. We should learn to accept what is beyond our capacity to change. It is the law of nature that day is followed by night. Joy and sorrow are part of the same package. We should recognize this truth. An elephant can never behave like a frog. A frog can never be an elephant. Accept them as they are—the elephant as an elephant and the frog as a frog. Know that sugar is sweet and that salt is salty. Learn not to jump sky high when happiness visits or become devastated when sorrow comes into our life. Remain content and joyful under any situation. This is what is meant by 'maturity.' This is what spirituality teaches us."

For enlightened beings such as Amma, Krishna and Jesus, spiritual knowledge is their experience. That armor is a natural part of them. However, we have to continue to put in steady effort to acquire and assimilate this wisdom. This doesn't mean we all have to become monks or ascetics. No matter who we are and what we do, we can all reserve a small portion of our day for spirituality. It may be reading a few pages of a spiritual book, listening to a talk on spirituality, reserving some time to reflect over a verse from the Bhagavad Gita, focusing and calming our mind through meditation, prayer or chanting our mantra. Amma assures us that the benefits that come from time spent in such activities is never wasted. All of them take us closer to the goal.

Amma says, "Spirituality teaches us how to be strong when facing any crisis and how to always maintain happiness and contentment. Spirituality helps us to deeply understand life and to maintain the right attitude towards it."

Regarding a person who possesses real wisdom, the Mahabharata says: *kuśalī sarva-dukheṣu sa vai sarva-dhano narah*—"Into whatever difficulties such a person may fall, he remains cheerful."[51]

---

[51] Mahabharata 12.226.23

Expectations Make us Suffer

Once, someone I was working with on a project said she would come by the next morning, as we had some work to do together. However, the next morning came and went, and she didn't come. Actually, in itself it didn't matter. I worked on something else instead. Still, I felt let down because I had expected her to come, and she hadn't. I felt like she didn't care. She hadn't bothered to inform me that she wasn't coming. I tried calling her, and she didn't pick up the phone.

Later, when I saw her, she explained that she had been busy with other work. When I asked her why she hadn't messaged me, she explained there was a problem with her phone. My irritation doubled after talking to her. For one, I had expected her to come and she hadn't. Secondly, I expected her to acknowledge she had let me down, instead of which she was simply blaming her phone. *She* was fine; *I* was irritated. I blew the situation out of proportion because my expectations hadn't been met. That's all it was—expectations. At the end of the day, I hadn't wasted any time and had accomplished other things.

In today's world it is difficult to live without expectations. That being the case, at least we can try to expect the negative as well as the positive. Amma gives an example: A man becomes bankrupt in his business. He decides to ask his well-off childhood friend to help him by lending him 200,000 rupees. He goes to him with great expectations. The friend may lend him 400,000 instead. He may lend exactly the requested amount. Or he may also lend only half of it. Alternatively, he might even say he is in a bad situation himself and lend nothing at all. If that happens, the man might end up feeling dejected or angry. Instead of expecting only the desired result, if he had approached his friend with an open mind understanding that there was a range of possible outcomes, he could have avoided the disappointment and frustration.

An incident in the Mahabharata illustrates how expectations can cause problems for even the best of people. It was well into the war. The great warriors Bhishma and Drona had fallen. Finding it difficult to face the Pandavas, Duryodhana asked Karna to lead the army. Karna agreed and immediately attacked Yudhishthira so fiercely that the Pandava leader was injured and forced to leave the battlefield. Yudhishthira felt humiliated.

As Arjuna's chariot, led by Krishna, moved towards Karna to attack him, Bhima appeared in their path. He called out to them, "Yudhishthira has been wounded and has left the battlefield."

Worried, Arjuna cried out to Krishna, "I have to see my brother. I can't fight until I have seen him."

Krishna drove the chariot away from the raging battle. Seeing them approach, Yudhishthira's face lit up as he assumed Arjuna had killed Karna in battle. He embraced Arjuna, "You have killed Karna! You've made us all proud, Arjuna. I was weighed down by fear, day and night, thinking of his might. Which weapon did you use? How did you kill him?"

Arjuna replied, "Brother, I haven't fought with Karna yet. Hearing you were wounded, we wanted to see you. With your blessings, I will kill Karna tomorrow without fail."

At these words, Yudhishthira lost his composure. He started reprimanding Arjuna. "I have agreed to wage this war with all my hopes on you. What is the use of having the mighty Gandiva bow when you can't stand before Karna? It's high time you should give your bow to Krishna, he will destroy the enemies. It's shameful to flee the battlefield!"

Arjuna, in turn, reacted in indignation and fury to his brother's words. In the end, the situation was saved by Krishna, who intervened and brought harmony back between the two.

The strength of the Pandava brothers lay in their unity. Still, under the pressures of war, even the relationship between Yudhishthira and Arjuna was strained. Yudhishthira was calm and composed by nature. As well-balanced as Yudhishthira was, he still became overwhelmed due to his expectations. He had expected Arjuna would have already killed Karna, putting an end to further bloodshed. He felt let down, and reacted in anger.

Amma says, "Expectations are what bring sorrow. When we don't get what we expected, we feel sad. This sadness gives way to anger, which ultimately leads to depression. But it all starts with expectations."

We can recollect moments in our life when we have lost our mental peace because of others. Moments when we have felt agitated, angry, sad, irritated, left out or let down. If we think about the root cause of those feelings, we'll realize that it was not the behavior of the other person in itself. Rather, our mental agitation sprang from our unmet expectations.

Imagine we want to share some good news with a friend or a family member. That news is very important to us. We have been waiting all day to tell them. Finally, when we excitedly share the news with them, they don't react in the way we had expected. They simply say, "Okay, good" and change the subject. Such things are enough to make us feel dejected. Or when we undergo some difficulty, we may turn towards various people hoping for empathy and support. Sometimes we may be disappointed with their reactions and end up feeling disheartened and alone.

Our sorrow is caused by our expectations. We expect love, support, empathy, care and trust. When those expectations are not met, we suffer and our relationships suffer too. Expectations blind us to the good in others and in ourselves. Because of my expectations, I created a train of negative thoughts towards my co-worker, who in reality hadn't done anything wrong. Because of his expectation, Yudhiṣṭhira couldn't see that Arjuna returned from the battlefield out of concern for him.

Amma says, "At present we lack the capacity to really love others because of our ego. We want others to tune to us, but we are unwilling to tune to others. Thus, the ego blocks the flow of real love. Love one another without any expectations. Then, there is no need to go anywhere in search of heaven."

This level of love may sound idealistic and beyond our reach. But Amma assures us that we *are* capable of such love. Love being our real nature, we can never lose it. At present, we cannot experience such love because, similar to the clouds covering the sun on a rainy day, our essence of divine love is covered by our desires and selfishness. Still, we needn't be discouraged. We can gradually drive those clouds away. As a first step, we can try to become aware of our expectations. Often, they are hidden, which explains our tendency to blame others for our suffering. If we try to identify our unhelpful expectations and understand how they hurt us, it becomes easier for us to let them go. Another effective method to weaken unhealthy expectations is to try to develop feelings of compassion and gratitude for the other person. We can try to put ourselves in their shoes and forgive them the way we all so easily forgive ourselves.

Titikṣā: Patient Forbearance

The Bhagavad Gita contains many powerful, timeless messages for humanity. A message that is particularly relevant in times of crisis is that of *titikṣā*—forbearance.

> *mātrā-sparśāstu kaunteya śītoṣṇa-sukha-duḥkhadāḥ*
> *āgamāpāyino'nityāstāmstitikṣasva bhārata*

> Contacts of the senses with their objects, O son of Kunti, give rise to the experience of cold and heat, pleasure and pain. Transient, they come and go. Forbear them, O Arjuna![52]

Hearing this, the image that may come to mind is that of a yogi standing on one foot in the Himalayas, absorbed in great austerities, oblivious to the surrounding cold. Such a person may have great forbearance and remain completely unperturbed. But for ordinary people like us, the pairs of opposites are a very real part of our daily life: pleasure and pain, attraction and aversion, hot and cold, likes and dislikes. Is it really possible to live in the world and not be affected by these? What does Lord Krishna mean when he advises us to have *titikṣā*? Is it really practical?

We can try to look at the concept of *titikṣā* through a little incident. Towards the beginning of the pandemic, one of my friends tested positive. The message she sent me that day was something like this: "I feel terrible. I have body pain and fever. Why is this happening to me? I have been so careful. I've been keeping to myself and always wear a mask when I go out. What

---

[52] Bhagavad Gita 2.14

if this becomes serious? I'm scared I'm developing breathing problems. I feel a kind of pressure in my chest. I'm so scared."

I tried to reassure her and told her not to panic. The next morning, I asked her how she was doing. This was her reply: "After chanting my archana[53] this morning, I felt better. Physically, I think my throat pain and body ache have gotten a bit worse. I still feel a little nervous about my health, but the situation feels less dramatic now. I don't feel so upset. Since I calmed down, I can breathe better too."

Notice the difference between the two messages. My friend was in a challenging situation. But on the first day, her fear and panic had gotten the better of her, making everything seem intolerable. Her reaction created extra suffering for her. But that changed the next day because of her shift in perspective. The external situation was the same, but she wasn't creating additional stress. This is what is meant by *titikṣā*.

Amma says, "Ten percent of life's experiences we have no control over, but the remaining 90 percent depend on our reactions to the first 10 percent. So, if we are able to respond rather than react in such situations, we can definitely turn things to our advantage. There is one thing we can always keep in check—our mental attitude. Let us try to be strong and optimistic."

Hearing this, some may ask, "But what about those of us who have experienced devastating loss? How can *titikṣā* apply then?" In such situations, we can get strength from what Lord Krishna says about the nature of human experiences: *āgamāpāyinaḥ*—"they come and go," they have a beginning and an end. However crushing grief may feel, it will pass. Everything in the world is transient, even overwhelming grief is no exception to the rule.

---

[53] The thousand names of the Divine Mother

Someone I know lost her adult son. Needless to say, her grief is unimaginable. But she says the reason she is able to get up each morning and keep courage is the thought that the intensity of this grief will pass, at some point. Life will move on.

Some of us face challenges that might not leave us, at least in this lifetime. Some have to live with chronic pain, be it psychological or physical. Others have a family member who causes them concern. In such cases, being able to bring our mind to a place of acceptance towards that which we cannot control is very helpful. It doesn't make the difficulty go away, but it enables us to gradually move away from thought patterns that reinforce our negative feelings towards the situation. Each time we try to establish ourselves in the present moment and feel some degree of peace with the situation, we further weaken our habit of creating stories that pull us down. Through such a practice of *titikṣā* we learn to be kind and compassionate towards ourselves. This gradually strengthens us to face the situation calmly and with courage.

Amma says, "There will be failures and sadness in each life. But we should not lose our courage, presence of mind and optimism while going through such phases. Even if we lose them, we should be able to regain these qualities in a short while. Many people sink into self-pity over minor setbacks, blaming others and living embittered lives. Yet, there are many who move forward with courage and optimism even in the midst of deep sorrow. Don't despair. Let's not allow the small flame of faith to get extinguished."

Life's challenges may feel tough at times. We may have lost someone who is close to us. We may be far away from our family members. We may have lost our job or be facing difficulties at work. We may struggle with depression or feelings of loneliness. Still, in such times, we can try not to lose heart. If we focus on trying to keep courage amidst sorrow, our attitude will be a source of strength and inspiration for the people around us also. It's not possible to change our outlook on life overnight. But if we keep trying, we can gradually increase our power of *titikṣā* and avoid adding unnecessary suffering through our thoughts. We can try to bear our hardships bravely, refusing to let darkness swallow us up. Though we may not see it now, there is light at the end of the tunnel.

The Weapon of Wisdom

After the Mahabharata War, on the Kurukshetra battlefield, Gandhari saw thousands of wives and mothers crying piteously over the bodies of their husbands and sons. She turned to Krishna and said, "Krishna, it is your fault! If you had wanted to, you could have stopped this war from taking place. You didn't bother. You could have calmed the enmity between the cousins. Rather, you chose to side with the Pandavas. You have brought the entire Kuru lineage to its ruin. I, Gandhari, curse you that your clan will also die the way my children have died. The men from your clan will fight among themselves and kill one another, down to the last one. And your women will weep then, as all of us do today! As for you, Krishna—you will die all alone. It'll be a common death, without any glory. I curse you for the deaths of all the Kaurava heroes!"

In reality, Krishna had wholeheartedly tried to stop the war. He had gone to the Kaurava assembly as a messenger of peace, as a last attempt to prevent the war. He always remained firmly established in dharma.

Even in the face of this false accusation and terrible curse, Krishna retained his smile. Neither was he disturbed in the slightest, nor did he hold any resentment towards Gandhari. That is because he knew the nature of the world and of the human mind. He knew what to expect.

Lord Krishna didn't need to try to imbibe great truths about the nature of the world. That knowledge was an inseparable part of his being. Therefore, he naturally didn't have any unrealistic expectations regarding the world. This is what allowed him to face a very challenging situation with graceful equipoise.

However, that is not the case for ordinary people like us. Amma says, "Sometimes, we may feel our mind is very peaceful. However, when a certain situation arises, anger stirs us to react thoughtlessly. Without reflecting for even a moment, we react. In adverse circumstances, what matters is how maturely and discriminately we can respond."

Once, I felt annoyed with a coworker. I had found myself in this situation with her previously, but for some reason, this time I felt particularly irritated. I knew from previous experience that there was no point in trying to complain to her. If I did, she would only make it seem like I was being dramatic, and I would end up feeling even more frustrated.

For the sake of my own peace of mind, I decided that I'd better not express my frustration to this person directly. Some friends were nearby, so I started telling them what had happened, hoping my frustration might reduce a little through venting. But—unfortunately—the person in question happened to come by at that moment. Even more unfortunately, I let something slip out of my mouth without thinking. I blurted out, "See, I'm complaining to them because I know there's no point in trying to talk to you directly."

Predictably, she replied, "Don't do that. Just tell me."

And that was it. What happened next was exactly what I had wanted to avoid. I started listing my complaints. She became defensive, and started justifying and denying. I ended up losing all my mental equanimity and left feeling angry and extremely frustrated.

But as I was walking away, I heard Amma's words in my head—words that I have heard countless times. Words that I have many a time used as advice for others. Words that I forgot when it came to putting them into practice. These are those words of Amma: "What matters is how maturely and discriminately we can respond to a situation."

It struck me that I had failed the test. Why had I acted like that? Because of my strong feeling of frustration. I had already experienced this aspect of that person's personality, and I knew she wouldn't accept any responsibility. So, why did I expect a different kind of behavior from her and get all worked up? It was clear that while I was fuming, she was completely fine and unaffected. I was the only one to suffer from my anger. She was getting on with her day unruffled.

We may know *theoretically* about the nature of the world and of the people around us. We may know that it's harmful to our well-being to have unrealistic expectations of others. But often this wisdom leaves us when we need it. It reminds me of stories from the Puranas,[54] when a warrior forgets the special mantra to invoke his celestial weapon. That always happens in the middle of the battle, at the time when they need it the most.

What is the remedy for this? How to make sure we have our knowledge-weapon when we need it, when challenging situations arise? That knowledge needs to become part of us.

Amma often talks of the importance of having a gap between our thoughts and actions. That gap creates an opportunity for the light of awareness to shine through, an opportunity to summon our own celestial weapons of knowledge and understanding. During the argument with my co-worker, if I had stepped aside and reflected for a moment, I could have behaved more maturely. I could have tried to understand her actions. Instead of anger, I could have tried to have consideration and sympathy.

---

[54] Ancient texts, containing many of the well-known Hindu stories

However, as we assimilate spiritual knowledge and make it our own, responding to situations in a mature way becomes natural for us. Amma says, "Reflection on spiritual truths must become a part of life, just as we eat, sleep and breathe. That will help us gain the strength to rise above challenging situations. Spirituality is not something to be practiced once in a while. It should be with us, in our hearts, all the time, like a dear friend."

Seeing the Right Way Up

Once a friend of mine told me a funny story. A few days before, a colleague had asked him for help with a technical glitch. The colleague was trying to join an important Zoom meeting, and his laptop kept freezing. My friend managed to get Zoom to work. A message then popped up on the screen asking to connect the microphone. He picked up a round black device on the desk and asked, "This is your mic, right?"
His colleague said, "No, no! That's the camera!" and showed him the microphone.

My friend put the camera back down, and connected the mic to the computer. Everything seemed to be set up correctly. They were ready to go. My friend joined the meeting, and clicked on the icons to enable the camera and mic. They both got a shock when the colleague's video appeared on the screen, alongside that of the other participants: it was upside down.

My friend immediately tried to adjust the position of the camera. But the image on the screen remained upside down. As the meeting was going on, he tried to fix the problem through various attempts. He went into the video settings. He tried unplugging and plugging the camera back in. But all was to no avail. The next step would be to restart the computer and reboot the system. By then the meeting was well underway, so it was not possible to exit the meeting and restart the computer. Therefore, his colleague ended up going through the entire meeting with his video upside down.

We both laughed as he recalled the situation. But the story also made me think. We all have a tool that we fall short of operating correctly at times. That is not a camera or mic, but a tool that we use throughout our life—day in, day out. That tool is our mind. As a result, frequently, our perception of a situation or of the world around us is "upside down." Our mind is like the camera through which we perceive the world. Naturally, a defect in this camera causes a corresponding defect in our perception.

Amma often reminds us that when we buy a new machine—like a blender—it comes with an instruction manual. We'll only know how to use the machine properly after reading the manual. For example, it'll tell us how to ensure the blender's engine doesn't overheat. We are all equipped with a complex tool, the mind—but we haven't been taught how to use it correctly.

Spirituality provides us with the user's manual for the mind. It gives us both knowledge and training to see everything in our day as an opportunity for growth. Like this, we gradually learn to view the world through the lens of gratitude and equanimity.

Duryodhana in the Mahabharata is a good example of someone who viewed the world "upside down." Through an evil plot and a fraudulent game of dice, the Kauravas exiled their cousins, the Pandavas, and their wife, Draupadi, to the forest for 12 years. During the last few years of their exile, the Pandavas lived in a forest called Dvaitavana.

Duryodhana, who was chiefly responsible for their plight, wanted to rub salt in the Pandavas' wounds. He set up an expedition to Dvaitavana, on the pretext of taking inventory of the kingdom's cattle. In reality he just wanted to show off, flaunting his wealth and power.

But things didn't end up going according to Duryodhana's plan. He and his wives were captured by gandharvas (celestial beings) who wanted to punish him for his arrogance. Ultimately it was the Pandavas who came to Duryodhana's rescue.

Yudhishthira's parting words before Duryodhana headed back to Hastinapura with his entourage were, "Go in peace; I wish you well."

Duryodhana could have felt thankful to the Pandavas. After all, Yudhishthira had treated him like a brother and saved him. Duryodhana could have taken the opportunity to make up with his cousins and restore their kingdom to them. He could have realized that, with their incredible strength and integrity, they would make excellent allies. He could have felt grateful towards life—despite his evil intentions, he had been spared and treated with respect.

Instead, Duryodhana sank into complete despair. He focused only on his sense of shame at having been helped by the Pandavas. In reality, life was treating him kindly. But his distorted vision made him feel that all odds were stacked against him. Rather than feeling supported, he felt that everyone was opposed to him—to such an extent that he even considered taking his own life.

We may think that we are nothing like Duryodhana. But in reality, there probably are situations in which our thoughts follow similar patterns. Sometimes, just a small challenge or difficulty is enough to plunge us into despair. At times our mood causes us to view everything as grim and we see everything in a negative light. At such times, we pull ourselves down and may also have a similar impact on those around us.

Amma says that our mind focuses on what we lack—or what is not according to our liking, similar to how the tongue goes to the space left by a missing tooth. Spirituality teaches us to see everything in its proper place, without giving undue importance to things that don't deserve it. Through this, spirituality trains us to develop gratitude, rather than focusing on negativity.

Amma says, "Gratitude is the ability to reminisce with humility about all the support and help we have received in life. It is a state of mind. When we lovingly recognize the goodness in another person, it helps awaken our own goodness. In fact, gratitude benefits us more than anyone else. The positivity and goodness that awaken within as a result of being grateful in turn benefit society and the entire world."

Unfortunately, we can't magically transform our outlook on life overnight. Sometimes, like Duryodhana, our mind zooms in on something negative and we see everything upside down as a result. Of course, it is not helpful to beat ourselves up over the negative thoughts we have. We all have such thoughts; they arise uninvited. But when that happens, the key is to try to let them go rather than dwelling on them.

Amma says, "Negative thoughts arise because it is time for them to disappear. Learn to see your thoughts like scenery passing by outside the window of a moving train."

The more we train our mind to view life with a spiritual outlook, the weaker and less frequent our negative thoughts will become. Gradually, we'll be able to see the world "the right side up"—through the lens of gratitude.

11

Spiritualize your Day

The Ishavasya Upanishad famously says, *īśāvāsyam idam sarvam*— "Everything in this universe is enveloped by God."[55] In the light of this, opportunities to connect with the sacred within are not restricted to time spent in a temple, church or mosque. Our spirituality gains depth when it expands to all areas of our day-to-day life. However we fill our days—at work or at home—we can use every activity to further our spiritual growth.

---

[55] Ishavasya Upanishad verse 1

Skill in Action

One morning, I reached the terrace to hang my clothes as usual, and there, right in front of me, was a cat. She was sitting in the middle of the terrace, looking at me. It looked like she had been waiting for someone to come. She immediately came to me and started going around my legs, purring. She then went a little further away and stood next to something. She looked at me expectantly. I went closer—she was standing next to a dead mouse.

I understood why she had been waiting for someone to come: She wanted to show off her achievement. It was the exhilaration of her catch that made her dance around me, purring with pride!

I laughed to myself, thinking that we behave just like that. When the result of our work comes as hoped, we are happy; we feel a glow of pride. And when others acknowledge it and appreciate it, we are beside ourselves with joy. There is nothing wrong with that in itself. It's natural. But at the same time, we need to remember that it shouldn't be our focus.

If we place too much emphasis on the results of our actions, we will not be able to maintain equipoise and mental peace when faced with failure. And failure is an unavoidable part of life, as much as success is. No one can change that.

Lord Krishna tells us in the Bhagavad Gita: *sukha-duḥkhe same kṛitvā lābhālābhau jayājayau*—"Treat good times and hardships, gain and loss, victory and defeat with equanimity."[56] This is one of the greatest messages the Bhagavad Gita gives

---

[56] Bhagavad Gita 2.38

to humanity. Ups and downs are the very nature of life. Sri Krishna goes on to tell Arjuna to "fight." He tells him this because Arjuna was a warrior, and in that context, taking part in the war they had tried—and failed—to stop was his duty. Through these words to Arjuna, Krishna is instructing all of us to persevere in our field of action. He instructs us to work to the best of our abilities without worrying about the results.

Amma says, "Perform your actions with care, without thinking and worrying about the results. The karma yogi[57] knows that the result of his actions are not in his control and that he is merely an instrument in God's hands. Therefore, he performs every action, no matter what, with utmost sincerity and accepts the outcome, whatever it is, as God's will. He does not become anxious about the fruits of his action."

I remember the first time I was asked to give a talk in Malayalam for Amrita TV. It was a short talk about my love for India. I was quite nervous and practiced it a lot—*a lot.* The filming took place, and a few weeks later it was broadcasted. Several people told me how much they liked it. With each new person who complimented me on my talk I became more and more elated.

Then I was asked to prepare another talk. The team hadn't understood how difficult Malayalam was for me. They overestimated my fluency and gave me the same amount of time to prepare as other speakers—two weeks. I tried to prepare the talk as fast as possible, but by the time I'd finished writing it, I had only a couple of days left to practice.

The TV crew, about eight people, came from Trivandrum and set up the studio. I was to be the first one of several speakers. I stood in front of the cameras and spotlights. It was only when we actually started recording that I realized how vital my extensive practice had been in the success of the first talk.

---

[57] A seeker who follows the path of karma yoga, the path of action

This time, my speech was more inconsistent and fumbling, and the producer kept having to stop me to correct my pronunciation. I ended up having to retake several paragraphs, and as a result the session took a lot longer than planned. The next speaker arrived for his recording when I was still far from being done with mine. Because of the delay, he had to sit outside and wait. I could feel the patience of the camera men and the rest of the team waning as we kept having to retake passages. The longer it took, the more nervous I became, and my nervousness then made me make even more mistakes.

Finally, it was over. At the end, the producer approached me and asked, "What happened? You did so much better last time!" I told her that I hadn't been able to practice enough. To top everything, the short drive back to the ashram from the studio made me feel car sick. I arrived home feeling queasy, quite miserable and sorry for myself. For the rest of the day, whenever I'd think back to the filming session, it was like revisiting a nightmare.

During the evening bhajans, I was still filled with dissatisfaction and disappointment. At one point it dawned on me how negative my state of mind was. I decided to try to come out of my self-pity and focus on the bhajans. Right then, Amma sang a song with the following lines: *sarvārpaṇa-bōdham nila-nilkkunnuṇḍ-eviḍe, garvaṅgaḷ akannīṭina śāntātmāv-aviḍe*—"Where there is total surrender, there is a soul filled with peace, devoid of all pride."[58]

I immediately realized that I had been completely out of tune with the bhajan's teaching. The idea of karma yoga[59] is to perform our actions to the best of our ability, and surrender the results to God—to the universe. Certainly, I had tried to do my

---

[58] *Svīkarichīḍū mama mānasa-pūjā*
[59] The path of action

best. But my happiness was now being dictated by the results of my actions. After the first filming had been successful and I had received appreciation and praise, I had soared to the skies in pride, a little like the cat purring with pride at her catch! After the second filming, when my actions had been met with criticism, I had sunk into the depths of self-pity.

I had created sorrow for myself by being overly attached to the results of my actions. Upon realizing this, my negative feelings about the morning's recording instantly lifted. I felt calm and relaxed: I had tried my best in both situations. The results were not for me to worry about; they were influenced by various other factors beyond my control.

As Lord Krishna says, *karmaṇyevādhikāraste mā phaleṣu kadācana*—"You have control over action alone, never over its fruits."[60]

Amma explains that performing our actions with an attitude of detachment towards the results doesn't mean acting without a plan or goal. That would be foolishness. Rather, it means we should try not to have expectations regarding the results. After all, many different factors influence the outcome of our actions, and the result may not turn out as we had desired. Performing our actions with such understanding is a way to protect ourselves from unnecessary sorrow and disappointment. Moreover, letting go of our concerns about the result frees up our mind, enabling us to focus better on the task at hand, giving it our best. The result of the action will come to us, whether we worry about it or not. Through shifting our focus from the results to the action itself, we allow our inner potential to be expressed.

——ᗧᗧᗧ——

---

[60] Bhagavad Gita 2.47

Love in our Work

One day, in Amritapuri, Amma was conducting a discussion regarding the attitude we should have towards work. Different people were taking the mic and sharing their thoughts on the matter. One German devotee offered a memorable perspective. She told us, "I was in Sri Lanka when the tsunami hit. When water came in, I was in no state to save myself. I couldn't even stand up by myself. So I relied fully on others to be saved. Only because of the help of others, I survived. That incident was quite a turning point in my life; my experience made a deep impact on me. After the tsunami, after getting back to my life in Germany, images of the tsunami haunted me. I kept thinking of the thousands of people who had lost their lives. And I felt a sense of guilt—guilt that I had survived when so many others had not.

"I felt a void in my life and work. I felt that since I had been allowed to survive, at least the remaining part of my life should be for the good of the world. My work was broadcasting for a radio station. Suddenly, it seemed empty and meaningless to me. My life seemed empty unless it could be of service. At the same time, I felt a little helpless—I had no idea what I could do to be of service to the world.

"One day I met a good friend and told her about the void I experienced and my frustration that my job wasn't one of service. My friend said, 'Why do you think your work cannot be one of service? If you do your radio-station work with love and sincerity, to the best of your capacity, it will become service.

Can you know how many people will be touched upon hearing your voice and the questions you ask during interviews?'"

The lady continued, "These words of my friend changed my outlook completely. They opened my eyes. I started to perform my work with as much love and sincerity as I could. I felt a sense of fulfillment, of meaning."

This story reminded me of something Amma says: "If we pour our heart and soul into an activity, it will be transformed into a tremendous source of inspiration. The product of an action performed with love has a discernible presence of light and life in it. That reality of love will fill people's minds with inspiration."

It doesn't matter so much what we do, but how we do it. What makes our life meaningful is not the scope or success of our actions. Rather, it is the care and attention we bring them, however small or insignificant those actions may seem.

Sage Agastya suggested to Rama that he spend the remaining years of exile in a place called Panchavati. Following these instructions, Rama, Sita and Lakshmana went there and reached a beautiful area near the Godavari River.

Rama took Lakshmana's hand in his and walked around Panchavati. The area was marked by five massive banyan trees. Rama selected an ideal spot for their home. It was atop a small hill. It wouldn't get flooded during the monsoon season. The area was perfectly clean. There was a scenic view of the mountains on every side. Birds of various colors flew here and there. The area abounded with fruit trees and flowering plants. On one side of their camp was a small stream, a tributary to the river. It was clearly an ideal place to stay.

Lakshmana began his work. He gathered various branches, grasses and leaves. He became completely absorbed in the construction. He leveled the floor and elevated it with a thick layer of clay. For the structure, he used bamboo poles as pillars. They would provide strong support, withstanding all kinds of weather. For the walls he used shami branches and jute strands. He insulated it with blades of kusha and other types of grass. Lakshmana worked on the hut with love and dedication. After several days, it was ready. He bathed in the Godavari and brought lotuses from the river. He offered the lotuses to the devatas[61] of the forest and chanted some mantras for warding off evil. He then approached Rama and Sita and told them the dwelling was ready. Rama walked over with him and admired the sturdy and delightful hut. Moved by Lakshmana's work, Rama's eyes filled with tears. He embraced his brother and said: "You have accomplished a great feat. O my brother, you do so much for me and all I can reward you with is an embrace."

What was the secret behind the beauty and perfection in Lakshmana's work? It was the love and sincerity he had poured into it. He was fully present when doing the task, giving it his best. Every branch, log and blade of grass was imbued with the love he had for his brother Rama.

Amma says, "Do your work and perform your duties with all your heart. Try to work selflessly with love. Pour yourself into whatever action you perform. Then you will feel and experience beauty and love in everything you do. Love and beauty are within you. Try to express them through your actions, and you will definitely touch the very source of bliss."

————⌣⌣⌣————

[61] gods or deities

Work as Worship

One way to bring love into our work is by doing it with an attitude of worship. This is bhakti—an important aspect of spirituality in Sanatana Dharma. Bhakti is love and devotion towards the divine. Ultimately, its goal is to lead us to an expansive vision of seeing the divine in everything. The similarities between expressions of love for God in different religious traditions is particularly inspiring. For instance, the poignant poems of Saint John of the Cross[62] are evocative of the songs of love written by Akka Mahadevi[63] and of the writings of Abu Sa'id.[64] Amma says that God is unconditional love. Love for God is, in fact, love for love's sake. This being a little abstract, it may be easier to direct our love towards a more tangible representation of God—a deity, the guru or an image. It can also be towards a divine quality such as compassion or light or towards nature. Ramana Maharshi famously revered Lord Shiva in the form of the Arunachala Hill. Bhakti is, in fact, love towards the Self manifested externally in order to help us discover the inner Self.

Once, a young girl came to Amma with a complaint. She wanted to study subjects linked to spirituality, like Sanskrit and the scriptures. Her parents, however, wanted her to study medicine. Amma explained to the girl that her path was to become a doctor. Trying to argue with Amma, she said, "But, Amma, I want to lead a spiritual life."

---

[62] Spanish Catholic priest and mystic
[63] Indian poetess and saint
[64] Persian poet, revered as one of the fathers of Sufism

Amma's reply was beautiful. It was a reply that is relevant for every one of us. Amma said, "A spiritual life isn't about doing only things related to Sanskrit, scriptures and formal spiritual practices. Rather, it is about making every aspect of our life spiritual."

In general, most people think spirituality only involves things like meditating, scriptural study, mantra chanting and contemplation. Some of us may think, it's all very well talking about the need for performing spiritual practices, but what if we don't have the time? We may think that monastics can talk about the importance of such things, but what about those of us who have a family to take care of, a job to go to, bills to pay?

However, Amma says, "Spirituality is not so much about *what* we are doing. It's more about *how* we do it."

We all tend to work with expectations. We work hard in our jobs expecting respect and appreciation from our colleagues and promotions from our boss. We sweep our yards and keep them neat, expecting our neighbors will notice. We work hard at school to get good grades, expecting a secure future. We cook delicious meals expecting appreciation and praise. We dress nicely, expecting compliments. So much of our life is based on expectations of future results.

When we harbor such a mindset, suffering is inevitable. Life will never live up to our expectations and even if our expectations are fulfilled and we obtain some satisfaction, it is only short-lived. Desires are endless, and the mind's next desire is just around the corner. This being the usual state of our mind, what can we do to try to align our attitude with spiritual principles?

In the Bhagavad Gita, Krishna says that whether we are aware of it or not, all of us are constantly performing actions. Sitting is an action, thinking is an action—even blinking is an action. Since actions are an inevitable part of being alive, we can try to reorient them and make them a path to our upliftment—a path to the divine. Lord Krishna indicates how we can go about this:

yat karoṣi yad-aśnāsi yajjuhoṣi dadāsi yat
yat tapasyasi kaunteya tat kuruṣva mad-arpaṇam

Whatever you do, whatever you eat, whatever you offer as oblation to the sacred fire, whatever you bestow as a gift, and whatever austerities you perform, O son of Kunti, do them as an offering to me.[65]

Amma says, "Perform every action as an offering to the divine, with *pūjā-manobhāva* (attitude of worship). Rather than trying to change the external situation, focus on changing your attitude. Our attitude changes the way we perceive a situation. When performing archana (chanting the names of the divine), we lovingly offer flowers with every mantra; we should try to offer our every action at the feet of the divine with the same devotional attitude. Like this, our every action can become a puja (worship)."

Several years ago I went to see an ayurvedic doctor. One small action of his made a deep impression on me. After writing the prescription, before handing it to me, he gently touched it to his forehead with reverence. I found this simple gesture inspiring. It introduced an element of grace, making the work feel sacred. In those days I was doing seva in the kitchen. I had shifts at the front counter, taking people's orders.

It was busy, and often the queue was very long. Since the work involved talking, I couldn't really chant my mantra. But, inspired by the ayurvedic doctor, I came up with an idea. Each

---

[65] Bhagavad Gita 9.27

time I'd take someone's order, I would try to make a point of mentally offering my action to God when I handed them their order-slip. I would do it for a few customers, and then I'd get distracted and forget all about it. I'd then remember and start again. Seeing how easily I'd forget, I started keeping track, as a reminder to myself. After giving a person their slip, if I had been able to mentally offer the action to God, I'd write a little tick on a paper. Like that, at the end of the shift, I'd be able to gauge my progress. Slowly, remembering the divine while handing people their order slip became a habit.

Amma says, "If you cannot find free time to devote to the worship of God, try to be like the gopis (the milkmaids of Vrindavan). They did not set aside a separate time for prayer. They saw God while immersed in their work. While selling dairy products, such as butter, curd and buttermilk, they would rename each item with various names of Krishna, such as 'Keshava,' 'Vasudeva,' 'Nandabala' and so forth."

If we try to transform *everything* we do each day into a puja overnight, we will fail and become disheartened. That's why it's helpful to take it one step at a time. We can begin by choosing one action in our day to wholeheartedly try to perform as puja. This could be anything—including brushing our teeth or making a cup of coffee. Then we can sincerely try to put it into practice during the next few days. It's not as easy as it sounds. Don't get disheartened if it takes several attempts before we develop the mindfulness to do it. Keeping a journal can be helpful to keep track of our progress. Once we have succeeded in bringing a devotional attitude to one particular action, we can add another. Like this, step by step, every moment of our day can be transformed into an offering of love.

Self-Confidence

An elephant has incredible strength. It can uproot an entire tree with its trunk. Yet the elephant remains in captivity, tied by only a light rope. Despite its ability to break its bonds, it doesn't even try. Why? Because it's first tied when it's small and not yet strong enough to break the rope. It will try to break free at first. It will try and try, but eventually realize it can't. Then, something binds it that is stronger than any rope or chain—the *belief* that it can't break free. It's this belief, or "conditioning," as Amma puts it, that holds the elephant back, despite its immense power.

Many of us have beliefs that hold us back. We doubt our capabilities. We may believe that we are not good enough, not strong enough. Not smart enough. Not brave enough. While it is true that some of these beliefs about ourselves may be true, many of them are imaginary ropes that hold us back from expressing our full potential.

Amma says, "Self-confidence is like a booster rocket. It is like fuel giving us the power to forge ahead."

Usually, I consider myself quite a confident person, but once an incident took place that showed me I still have a long way to go. I was asked to give a few talks to a group of students. I gave the first talk and felt it had gone well. The next day, I received a phone call from one of the organizers. I was in a meeting, so I couldn't take the call. Ten minutes later, I received a message from another organizer asking to speak to me as soon as possible. I was still in the meeting, so I couldn't call to find out what it was about.

In that space of unknowing, a little demon of self-doubt arose in my mind. It started saying, "Oh, they must have not liked your talk. They probably want to cancel the next one and have another speaker instead." I started doubting I'd been professional enough. "Most likely the in-charge doesn't want to tell you directly; that's why he is asking other organizers to talk to you." I began thinking how I'd told several of my friends about these talks and I'd have to tell them that they have now been canceled.

How slyly self-doubt can creep into our mind! The moment I stepped out after the meeting I called the organizer, ready to hear the bad news. It turned out that my insecurity had been completely unfounded. Actually, they were calling to request me to give an additional talk, for a different batch of students.

Thinking back on my thought processes during the meeting, I laughed at my stupidity. Amma says that the nature of the mind is to flow downwards, like water. It is so true. The problem is that our beliefs about our limitations can really hold us back. As a result, we often refrain from coming out of our comfort zone, even if it is to do something we really want to do.

After their 12-year period of exile in the forest, the Pandavas were to spend one year in hiding. Accordingly, they lived incognito in the court of King Virata, king of the Matsya Kingdom (neighboring the Kuru Kingdom). As the Pandavas' stipulated time in concealment was drawing to a close, the Kaurava army, led by Duryodhana, launched an attack in the south of the Matsya Kingdom. King Virata and his army fought back and were able to defeat the Kauravas. But before the victorious King Virata returned to the palace, news arrived that the Kauravas had invaded the kingdom in the north as well. Until King Virata's return, the court was under the care of the young and inexperienced crown prince named Uttara Kumara.

Uttara Kumara set off with Arjuna—whom he knew as Brihannala[66]—as his charioteer. Arjuna was eager to meet his adversaries, and the chariot raced forward at full speed. From afar, the Kaurava army looked like an ocean of soldiers. Beholding the vast army spread out ahead, Uttara Kumara started feeling nervous.

Uttara begged Arjuna to turn the chariot around, but Arjuna wouldn't. Finally, he jumped off the chariot and started running back. Arjuna caught the prince by the shoulder. He said, "My dear Uttara Kumara, it does not befit a warrior to flee the battlefield!" Arjuna then revealed his real identity to Uttara. The prince was astounded to find out that his sister's singing and dance teacher was, in fact, the valiant Arjuna. They proceeded to collect Arjuna's Gandiva bow from its hiding place and set off to battle. Uttara drove the chariot and Arjuna fought single-handedly. He ended up defeating the Kauravas in a heroic way.

There are moments in our life when we identify with Uttara Kumara—seeing a potentially challenging situation, we feel like running away. But within all of us, there is also an Arjuna. That Arjuna is our *ātma-viśvāsa* (self-confidence—literally, "faith in self"). Amma says, "Without self-confidence you cannot succeed in life, irrespective of your field. Self-confidence is nothing but mental balance, courage, and control over your own mind to confront the problems of life."

We can't expect to always meet with success. Thus, we also need to learn to be at ease with failure. How we deal with failure is of utmost importance. In times of failure, naturally we become more vulnerable to self-criticism. This in turn can

---

[66] During the Paṇḍavas' year of hiding, Arjuna was disguised as Brihannala, a eunuch who taught dancing and singing to princess Uttara, prince Uttara Kumara's sister.

damage our confidence in ourselves. That's why, to build our self-confidence in such situations, we need to become our own coach, rather than pulling ourselves down further.

To become a good coach for ourselves, we can imagine what our guru would tell us in such situations. The guru is fully aware of our weaknesses and strengths. By trusting in our abilities and encouraging us to go beyond our comfort zone, the guru awakens the Arjuna in us. That Arjuna defeats the enemies of our self-doubt, shyness and insecurity. That Arjuna breaks the imaginary shackles that we ourselves have created. This is one way the guru kindles self-confidence in us.

For those who don't have a guru, a technique used in Compassion-focused Therapy (CFT) offers a similar alternative. In this technique, you imagine a "perfect nurturer." That is a being who is completely committed to your growth and happiness—someone who embodies the qualities of wisdom, strength and unconditional love. You are then to imagine what advice the nurturer might give you.

Imagining the words of wisdom—be it from the guru or from a loving nurturer—helps silence our internal voice of self-criticism and doubt. Like this, we can gradually build our self-confidence, step by step.

———◯◯◯———

Awareness in Action

After many years of apprenticeship, a Buddhist monk thought he should be elevated to the category of teacher. One rainy day, he journeyed to visit his master. When he walked into the house, the master greeted him with a question.

"Tell me, did you leave your sandals and umbrella on the porch?"

"Yes," replied the disciple.

"And tell me," the master continued, "Did you leave your umbrella to the left or to the right of your sandals?"

"I have no idea," replied the monk.

The master said, "We need total awareness in *all* actions. The lack of attention to the smallest details can completely destroy a man's life. A samurai who doesn't take care of his sword every day, will at some point find it is rusty, just when he needs it the most."

The monk realized that he had not yet attained full awareness. He remained as a student under his master for ten more years.

Amma says, "Lack of awareness creates obstacles on the path to eternal freedom. It is like driving through the fog. You won't be able to see anything clearly. It is dangerous too, as an accident can occur at any time. On the other hand, actions done with awareness help you to realize your innate divinity. They help increase your clarity moment by moment."

We may think, so what if we don't remember exactly how we left our shoes? We sometimes don't realize how unaware we are of what's taking place in our mind. When thoughts or feelings come up, we tend to get carried away by them. Think of the all-too-common scenario when trying to meditate: We try to keep our focus—on our breath, on our mantra, or on whatever it may be. At one point, we remember with slight irritation a criticism someone had made about our work the previous week. Our mind immediately starts listing the reasons why that criticism was unjustified. With resentment, we embark on a train of thoughts regarding the person who was the source of the remark. Suddenly, we realize that 20 minutes have passed! Not only have we "missed" most of our meditation time, but our mind has by itself created a mood of dissatisfaction.

We can avoid such patterns through developing awareness. Amma says we do not have control over the first thought that arises in our mind, but we can decide what happens next: Do we pursue it and allow it to become a whole train of thoughts, or do we notice it, and simply let it go? Only if we have the alertness to notice that first thought will we be empowered to nip in the bud the unhelpful ones. It takes a lot of practice to develop such awareness, because the mind can be quite a trickster. One step towards developing alertness within is to cultivate it externally, by first learning to become aware of our actions and surroundings.

I often try to have awareness in my actions. And actually, I like to think that I *do* have a reasonable level of awareness. For example, I feel some pride in how neat and tidy I keep things. Once, I was helping an elderly ashram resident come to the Kali temple to receive Amma's darshan. We were coming up the steps of the temple. But some people had left their footwear in a very disorganized way on the steps. This made it more difficult for the elderly lady to walk. I frowned, thinking, "Can't these people have some awareness in their actions? Someone should tell them the story of the monk and his umbrella!" Anyway, it wasn't a big deal. I pushed the shoes aside and we continued up the steps.

A few days later, I was helping the same ashram resident come to the main hall to attend the evening bhajans. I offered one arm to the elderly lady to hold as support. With my other arm I held her cushion, and my computer bag was hanging on my shoulder. We reached the hall, and I helped her to a chair. I tried to make her comfortable with the cushion supporting her back. The satsang that usually takes place before bhajans had already started. I was about to sit down to listen when I realized I couldn't find my phone. I searched the compartments of my laptop bag. It wasn't there. In my rush, I must have left it in the room.

I told the lady, "Mother, I left the phone in the room. I'll leave my bag with you, get the phone and come back fast." I set off at a brisk pace. As I walked away, I thought, "Wait! I can still listen to the satsang online." I reached in my pocket, pulled out my phone and without slowing down the pace, opened the phone case and connected to the live-stream. I held the phone close to my ear and started listening to the talk.

All of a sudden, it dawned on me—I stopped right in my tracks. What a fool I was being! I was heading to my room to collect my phone, all the while holding that very phone to my ear. I was so shocked that I laughed to myself for a second before turning around and retracing my steps.

I thought of an elderly man I know who can be a little forgetful in his old age. When he does something absent minded, I've heard him exclaim, "Oh, my 80-year-old brain!"

But what excuse did I have? All I could think of was that, as it was only recently that my clothes had been fitted with a pocket, I was still not completely in the habit of using the pocket or checking it. But in the light of the absurdity of my action, that was quite a feeble excuse.

I reached the hall and, slightly embarrassed, told the elderly lady about my blunder. She gave me an astonished look and we both laughed.

Still smiling to myself, I sat down. "How could I have acted so absentmindedly? Maybe I'm not as aware of my actions as I like to think I am." I remembered how judgmental I had been about the footwear on the temple steps a few days before. Maybe I should start looking at my own awareness—or absence of it!—before pointing the finger at others.

After bhajans one day, Amma said, "We should try to develop awareness in every movement. That is real *sādhana* (spiritual practice). When bathing, when eating, when cooking—everything we do should be done with awareness. We have little or no awareness. Therefore, we are only partially present or not present at all. Spirituality teaches us to be fully in the present moment, irrespective of time and place."

It's impossible to switch to having awareness in all our actions overnight. But we can start implementing it in little steps, gradually. How we keep our shoes and umbrella may be a good place to start.

12

Spring Cleaning

Aham brahmāsmi—"I am the Supreme." This is one of the famous *mahāvākyas* (great sayings) from the Upanishads.[67] It means that the consciousness that is the essence of the individual is the same consciousness that is the essence of the totality. In other words, our true nature is divine. This is our eternal reality, but most of us are unaware of it because the state of our mind prevents our inner light from shining forth. Amma compares our mind to the glass enclosure for a traditional Indian oil lamp, which has to be kept clean so the sacred light can shine out. Our minds have become blackened with soot—neither can the light within shine out, nor can the light outside come in. This "blackening" is due to our inner impurities such as intense likes and dislikes, selfishness and pride. Thus, a key component of spirituality is the process of cleaning our mind to allow our inner divinity to manifest.

---

[67] Portions of the Vedas dealing with Self-knowledge

The Divine Cleaner

Once, I was speaking to my parents on the phone. They didn't have any major news, so after the initial "How-are-you-doings," our conversation gravitated towards their vacuum cleaner. My mother said, "Do you remember our old vacuum cleaner? It was so heavy and difficult to use. So, the other day, on my sister's recommendation, we finally went out and bought a new one. I wanted to try it out immediately, so I vacuumed the sitting-room. The vacuum was lightweight and easy to use. When I opened the part where the dust gets collected, I was surprised to see it was three-quarters full. I told your dad, 'I think we have been sold a second-hand vacuum cleaner! It must have been used already. Look, it's already full.' I was outraged that the shop had sold us a used vacuum, that too without telling us. But I still wanted to carry on. I emptied the dust, and went to the bedroom. When I finished, I opened the vacuum dust-bag again. Guess what? It was almost full again!

"At that moment I understood that we hadn't been ripped-off. It hadn't been used previously after all. All that dirt had come from those two rooms of our house. It's only then that we realized what a poor job our old vacuum cleaner did. Though the room would seem clean after vacuuming, so much dirt must have remained in the carpet. Now the house is getting a real cleaning. Dirt built-up over years is filling our new vacuum."

We laughed, thinking of how my mother had initially been so certain they had been ripped-off. After the phone call, I was thinking about the incident and was reminded of Amma's words: "After sweeping a room, it may look clean. But if we then wipe it with a wet cloth, a lot more dirt will come off. Similarly, we may not see the 'dirt' in our mind, but the guru creates situations that bring out the negativities hidden within."

When Amma says this, she doesn't necessarily mean that one person—the guru—*literally* creates situations for another person's growth. The concept of "guru" is often misunderstood. The guru is devoid of ego, and therefore has no interest or agenda of their own. The guru exists solely for the spiritual upliftment of those with whom they come into contact. The guru *seems* like a person because they have a body. In reality, the guru is not a limited person or individual. The guru is a principle—the principle that removes the darkness within us. (Etymologically, "gu - ru" means "the remover of darkness.") Being devoid of ego, the guru is as Amma says, like an empty pipe through which the entire universe flows.

Moreover, the guru doesn't necessarily have a personal form. Sanatana Dharma assures us that when a sincere thirst to awaken arises within a seeker, the universe becomes a teacher, taking as many forms as required. That is why the Srimad Bhagavatam tells us of the story of Dattatreya, who saw human beings, animals and entities in nature as his gurus. This being said, most of us lack the subtlety of mind to perceive the guru-principle in the world around us, and we need the tangible guidance of a guru in a personal form.

Ancient scriptures tell us that the essence in all is one. Our Self is the same as the Self of the guru. The difference is that the guru knows this fully—a guru experiences this truth every moment. Therefore, our bond with the guru is not a bond with someone external to us. Rather, it is our bond with our own true Self—the divine essence within. Love for and surrender to the guru is in reality love for and surrender to our higher Self. Ultimately this path leads us to shedding our self-centeredness. It is when we put down the burden of our ego that we see the unity and fundamental interconnectedness of everyone and everything.

The guru is the principle in creation that guides us, through innumerable ways, to this truth. The disciple is encouraged to see everything that happens to him or her as coming from the guru. Through this, the disciple remains open and receptive, and can learn and grow from every situation.

In the ashram, one afternoon, Amma was to come to record some new bhajans. There is a particular place where I usually sit during such recording sessions. I am quite attached to that place as I get a nice view of Amma singing. However, that particular day, two swaminis asked me to let someone else sit there. There was a good reason, and considering the situation, it was clearly the sensible thing to do.

Amma came, and I went to sit in the back. From there, I could barely see Amma. Rather than accepting the situation in a graceful way, my mind started grumbling. Without even realizing it, I slid into a pit of self-pity: "No one has any consideration for me at all. Who even cares whether I can see Amma or not?" I'm not very good at hiding my emotions, so I'm sure I must have had quite a sulky expression. Luckily, any potential damage was averted by my COVID face mask!

Later on, after the recording session, I was sitting in the main hall for bhajans. This is often a time of reflection for me. It was only then that a ray of light made its way through the thick clouds of negativity in my mind. It occurred to me that this was a situation to teach me something—a situation coming from the guru. I realized how immature my reaction had been. My ego had reared its head at the slightest prick.

Also, my reaction had revealed that I had a sense of entitlement towards the place where I usually sit. I considered it "my" place. Rather than recognising that what my sisters suggested was the correct course of action, I was holding it against them. In my expectation of consideration and respect, I myself had forgotten to give consideration and respect. I understood I hadn't exactly passed the test with flying colors—but now I felt grateful for the situation, which had revealed my ego and taught me a lesson.

Actually, the universe teaches us all the time. All experiences we go through in life are lessons—lessons about the impermanence of everything external, lessons about the risks of having too many expectations, lessons about the fulfillment that comes from giving. But until we connect with the *guru-tattva*—the guru principle—we are mostly unable to recognize and assimilate these lessons. We lack clarity regarding the obstacles that block the expression of our inner potential, the expression of our real nature. That is why through the ages, masters from all faiths have lived amongst us, sharing their teachings and guiding us compassionately.

Amma says, "Like the filter that purifies water, the guru purifies our mind. The guru removes our ego. We become slaves to our ego as we encounter each circumstance in life. We do not move ahead with discernment. When the ego raises its head inside us, we are incapable of perceiving and destroying it. In order to become capable, we need to surrender to the guidance of a guru."

In August 2000, the day after the UN Millennium World Peace Summit, a press conference was held with Amma. One of the journalists asked Amma: "What would you do if you ruled the world?"

Amma laughed and responded, "I would be the sweeper."

The journalist looked at her quizzically, and Amma explained with a laugh, "I would sweep everyone's mind clean."

The Envy Disease

Once, I saw a little girl throw a piece of idli[68] at a crow. The crow caught the piece in his beak. Then along came another crow. The little girl threw a second idli piece for the newcomer. Seeing another piece being thrown, the first crow dropped the piece he had in his beak and rushed forward. He caught the second piece, but had dropped his first catch in the process. The little girl looked at me and said, "Chechi,[69] did you see how foolish this crow is? The first piece was a little bigger, and now he has lost it."

Normally, crows are generous. When they find something to eat, they call their friends to share with them. This must have been an unusually jealous crow. The thought of what another crow might get made him forget about what he already had.

This can happen to us too. When we focus on what others have, we compare ourselves to them. We feel envious of anyone more skillful, wealthy, beautiful or popular than we are. Focusing on what others have and what we lack, we forget to appreciate what we have. Amma says, "A person who constantly compares himself with others is always thinking about other people. Never content or happy, he cannot experience the real joy of life."

A friend of mine told me an anecdote from her childhood. She used to feel jealous of her cousin's family because, in her eyes, they had everything. They were very wealthy: a huge house, swimming pool, trampoline, the latest video games and all the

---

[68] Steamed rice cake
[69] "Elder sister" in Malayalam

newest gadgets. My friend and her siblings were always excited to stay with their cousins. At the same time, they felt jealous because they didn't have such things themselves. They felt their cousins had an ideal life—the perfect family in the perfect home.

It's only when she grew older that she realized that, in reality, it was far from an ideal family. Her cousins lacked the most important thing: parents who loved each other, who were kind and respectful of each other. Their father was an alcoholic, and often abused their mother, who was at her wits' end. Dazzled by their house and luxuries, my friend and her siblings failed to notice any of this.

When she understood the truth of the situation it was a real eye-opener. It shattered her illusion that material objects were the most important thing. In the end, the roles reversed; her cousins wanted to come and stay at her family's house, because it had stability and love.

What happens in envy? We compare ourselves with others, but the comparisons are typically based on misunderstandings. We weigh our life against what we *imagine* someone else's to be. It may turn out that the people we are envious of actually have a lot of suffering in their life. The picture we have of someone's life may be very different from reality.

When we focus on what others have, we fail to appreciate the value of what we have. My friend hadn't realized the invaluable treasure her family had—that of a stable and loving atmosphere.

One of the most prominent examples of envy in our scriptures is Duryodhana, the Kaurava crown-prince. Witnessing the glory of his cousin Yudhishthira's elaborate Rajasuya sacrifice,[70] his jealousy literally made him sick. He could think of nothing other than the prowess of his Pandava cousins and their huge wealth of gold, pearls, emeralds, cows, camels and horses.

---

[70] Sacrifice ritual that marks the consecration of a great emperor

Duryodhana forgot about his own fortune. He was the de facto king of Hastinapura. He possessed all the comforts and luxuries of his kingdom: vast wealth, umpteen number of beautiful women and a huge army of soldiers. Blinded by jealousy, he could see none of that. He told his father, "I cannot cherish my wealth when I see the wealth of Yudhishthira. It is making me sick."

Envy is not about others but about ourselves—our lack of contentment. Amma says, "Comparison can be very destructive and can affect every aspect of life. Keep in mind that you cannot be someone else and that no one else can be you. You can only be you."

We may not have the extreme envy-sickness Duryodhana suffered. At the same time, if we observe our mind carefully, we may notice times when the success of others causes us to have negative feelings or thoughts. The first step is to have the subtlety to recognize this. We can then try to reexamine what we have with new eyes—eyes of appreciation and gratitude. A genuine effort to value what we have naturally brings about a sense of contentment. Over time, we will be able to develop the quality that Sage Patanjali, in the Yoga-Sutras, calls *mudita*—the broadmindedness to be happy at the happiness of others.

—⌣⌣⌣—

Cleanse the Mind

Amma says, "If we want to see our reflection clearly in a mirror, we first have to wipe away all the dust and grime from the mirror's surface. Similarly, in order to see our true nature in the mirror of our mind, we first have to remove all the impurities currently collected within it."

What are these impurities? They are the elements within us that rob us of our peace. They include pride, low self-esteem, anger, envy, intolerance and preoccupation with what others are thinking. Ultimately, all of these stem from our ego, our self-centeredness. The first step in getting rid of our mental negativities is to become aware of them. For instance, if we introspect, most of us will notice a habit of creating stories about what is going on in other people's minds. We have a tendency to imagine what others think about us. Not only is it unhealthy to dwell on how others view us, but also, much of the time, our conclusions are wrong.

One day I sent a message to a friend asking her about a certain matter. After two days, she still hadn't responded. I thought, "Oh, maybe she is upset with me for some reason, that's why she hasn't replied." A day or two later, I crossed paths with this person's sister. I was going to say hello, but she turned her head in the other direction. I thought again, "My friend really must be mad at me; she has obviously complained about me to her sister too."

I saw my friend a couple of days later and asked her why she hadn't replied to my message. It turned out I had been completely wrong. She had just been busy and had forgotten about my message. When I told her that I had thought she was upset with me, she was appalled. Like this, the mind can fabricate stories out of the smallest incident, and our interpretation of other people's behavior towards us is often wrong.

Robert Cleck, a psychologist at Dartmouth College, conducted an experiment. A realistic-looking scar was pasted on the faces of the participants. They were told that the purpose of the experiment was to see how strangers reacted to them, given they had very visible scars on their faces. For that, they were to have a conversation with a stranger in the next room. Before each participant left the make-up room, the experimenter would put away the mirror and say, "Let me just do a final touch-up on the scar to make sure it doesn't smudge." Rather than touching it up however, the experimenter would remove the scar completely. But the participants had no idea. They still thought they had the dramatic-looking scar on their face. They then would leave to have their conversation with a stranger.

When the participants returned, the experimenter would ask them how the conversation went. The replies of the participants were all along similar lines: "It was so awkward. The person kept staring at the scar on my face. And they wouldn't make eye contact at all! Their behavior made me feel so uncomfortable."

The participants completely misinterpreted what had happened. In reality, we all do this. We project various thoughts and opinions on the people around us and forget that our guesses are probably quite removed from reality.

An incidence of this is described in the Ramayana. Rama, Sita and Lakshmana were enjoying a peaceful morning in

Chitrakuta[71] when suddenly they heard the tremendous noise of an army approaching. Upon Rama's request, Lakshmana climbed a tree to get a better view. He saw an army approaching, abounding in horses and chariots. When he realized the army was led by their brother Bharata, he was filled with anger. He called down to Rama standing below: "My dear brother, take Sita to a safe hiding place. As for you, string your bow and be ready to fight. Having secured the throne of Ayodhya and clearly wanting undisputed sovereignty, Bharata, son of Kaikeyi, is coming ready to kill us."

Lakshmana then proceeded to say that Bharata deserved to be killed. In reality, Bharata's journey to the forest was motivated by the purest and noblest of feelings. He wanted to try to convince Rama to return to Ayodhya and be crowned king. Yet, seeing Bharata approaching, Lakshmana projected the cruelest intentions on him. Fortunately, Rama was there to correct Lakshmana's wrong thinking. In the absence of that, a bitter battle could have ensued.

Lakshmana's misconception came from his desire to protect Rama at any cost. On the other hand, Rama had a clear mind and was therefore able to stand back and view the situation with clear eyes. When we are too emotionally involved in a situation, we are usually unable to analyze it properly or to accurately interpret the behavior of the other person.

If we introspect, we'll notice this tendency to jump to false conclusions. Becoming aware of it is the first step in stopping this bad habit. The next is to try to stop caring so much about what other people are thinking.

---

[71] Their dwelling place during the first eleven years of their exile in the forest

Amma says, "When you develop patience and attentiveness, your internal mirror, which helps you to see and remove the impurities within yourself, becomes clear of its own accord."

Once we recognize this disposition of our mind, it becomes easier to tell it to be quiet before it jumps to negative assumptions. With a mind that stays quiet when needed, our counterproductive worrying will reduce, and our relationships will flourish.

The Baggage We Carry

There is a little girl from France who lives in the ashram. At the time of this incident, she was only about five years old. One day, during the evening program with Amma in the ashram main hall, she raised her hand and took the mic. She had two questions for Amma. This was the first question: "Amma, sometimes I feel very angry. In those moments, what can I do to stop feeling anger?"

Everyone can benefit from the answer Amma gave, "Just think, what do you want to gather as you go through the journey of life? Do you want to accumulate anger, jealousy, fear and enmity? Or do you want to cultivate good qualities—qualities such as compassion, patience, love and tolerance?"

This reminded me of a funny story. When my parents were young, they went on a trip with some friends to spend a few days close to the sea. The morning of the planned departure, one member of the group had a problem with his bag—the zipper broke. To prevent his belongings from falling out, he placed his bag inside a trash bag. He then tied up the trash bag.

They all put their luggage near the van. My father loaded all the bags into the boot. They then got into the van and set off, happy to be together and enthusiastic about their little trip. After a few kilometers, someone said, "Is it just me or does something smell bad?" They all agreed. It was like the smell of food gone bad. But no one could figure out where it was coming from. So, they rolled down all the windows and continued on their journey. When they reached their destination, they unloaded the luggage. It was then that they realized what had happened. When the friend whose bag's zipper had broken went to collect his luggage, he got a strong whiff of the bad odor they had all smelled during the journey. One touch and his fear was confirmed: instead of his luggage, they had loaded a bag of rubbish that had been kept out on the pavement for collection. They all had a good laugh at the situation. My parents' friend managed without his bag for the weekend, and since then, the incident has been a source of entertainment for many.

There is a valuable lesson for us in this story. As Amma said to the little French girl, we are all on the journey of our life, and it is up to us what luggage we take along. Do we want to develop good qualities, qualities that uplift us and the people around us? Or do we want to accumulate anger, fear, selfishness and jealousy?

In the 16th chapter of the Bhagavad Gita, Lord Krishna talks about two kinds of qualities: *āsurī sampad* and *daivī sampad*—demonic and divine qualities. Both divine and demonic qualities co-exist within each of us. These are not some extraordinary qualities that we have yet to discover. They are traits with which we are very familiar—traits of our character that determine our thoughts, words and actions. *Daivī sampad* are the qualities that uplift us. *Āsurī sampad* are those which pull us down. As Krishna explains: *Daivī sampad vimokṣāya nibandhāyāsurī matā*—"Daivī sampad is known to bring liberation.[72] Āsurī sampad is considered to bring bondage."[73]

We can't overestimate the importance of striving to cultivate good qualities. This is the way to find real contentment and peace. We can experiment and see the truth of Krishna's statement for ourselves. We feel happiest when we have feelings of love, gratitude, compassion, humility, and self-confidence.

---

[72] Liberation from all bondage, the eradication of all sorrows.
[73] Bhagavad Gita 16.5

Negativities such as impatience, low self-esteem, jealousy and fault-finding prevent us from experiencing peace of mind. These inner enemies pull us down. It's because of them that we are unable to realize our true potential and experience fulfillment. We may not be able to prevent the arrival of these inner enemies but once they arrive, we can control how long they stay. It is up to us whether we dwell on and thereby fuel them, or whether we try to reject them and respond to the situation in a mature, compassionate manner.

Amma says, "Each of us has the power to be a god or a demon. We can be Krishna or Jarasandha.[74] Both qualities are within us: love and anger. Our nature will be determined by which qualities we choose to nurture. So, we need to cultivate good thoughts, free from any spirit of anger, and a clear mind, free from conflict."

Let us move on to the little girl's second question. She said, "What should we visualize when Amma calls out, 'Mātā rānī ki jai' at the end of bhajans?"[75]

Amma replied, "You should imagine that you are cheering for the victory of the good over the evil within you. 'Mātā rānī's victory' represents the victory of good qualities—love, compassion, tolerance, patience, enthusiasm, positive faith—over the darkness of selfishness, jealousy, intolerance and despair."

Here Amma indicates that the initial step towards developing these good qualities is to desire them and pray for them in the first place. So, let us try to recognize that developing good qualities and coming out of our selfishness is the key to our happiness. Such understanding is the wisdom that protects us from going through our lives gathering a rubbish bag full of

---

[74] The powerful and unrighteous king who ruled the land of Magadha in Krishna's time

[75] Typically, at the end of the last bhajan, Amma calls out "Mātā rānī ki jai," which means "Victory to the Divine Mother."

negativities. Instead, we can try to develop qualities of patience, compassion, tolerance and love, and make goodness victorious within our heart.

13

Trust in Life

Lord Krishna's last instruction in the Bhagavad Gita is *mām ekaṁ śaraṇaṁ vraja*—"Surrender unto me."[76] This means, "Surrender to the divine that pervades this universe and also dwells within you." Surrender your limited self—your fears, selfishness and pettiness—to your true Self. The Gita says that aligning our thoughts, words and actions with this spirit of surrender ultimately leads us to self-realization. Putting effort in that direction also brings immediate and tangible benefits to our general well-being in our daily life.

---

[76] Bhagavad Gita 18.66

Carefree, Like a Child

One morning I had a surprise. When I looked at my phone, there was a message from my best friend when I was 10 years old. We were neighbors in a small village and went to school together. It was the first time I had heard from her in over 20 years. Along with the message was a photo of us playing at her house. The message read: "I came across this when I was sorting through my photos. This picture reminds me of some of the happiest times of my childhood. I feel so much nostalgia when I see it. I like to visit the village where we grew up. It brings back beautiful memories, memories of childhood—a simple and carefree life. I hope all is well with you! I'd be very happy to hear your news. With love."

My friend's message made me reflect. Childhood is a time we often look back on with some nostalgia. Of course, not everyone has the good fortune of a happy, carefree childhood. But deep down, many of us long for that special quality in our lives, similar to that of a small child who has no worries, trusting fully that everything will be taken care of by its mother. It is because the child has no worries that it can be fully in the present moment.

Sometimes we don't realize that we can enjoy the same childlike lightheartedness even in the more complicated days of adulthood, through surrender to the divine. With an attitude of genuine surrender, we can shoulder great responsibilities and at the same time remain more or less relaxed.

Amma tells a story: "Once the king of a country went to his guru to seek advice and solace. He was very tense and disturbed by many problems facing the country. He had lost all his mental peace. He even wanted to relinquish his throne to be relieved of his responsibilities. He told all this to his guru, pouring his heart out to him.

The guru said, "Fine. I will tell you what to do. Make an agreement to hand over the entire kingdom to me." The king gladly agreed. He made a formal announcement to this effect. Once it was done, the guru said, "Now the kingdom is mine. I hereby appoint you as its caretaker. You should govern it as my official representative."

The king, ever obedient to his guru's words, agreed. He returned to the palace and continued to rule. But now his mindset was completely different. He felt a great relief. He was no longer the king as the guru was now the ruler of the country. He was only an instrument in the hands of his guru. Therefore, he felt totally free from the burden of responsibilities that weighed him down before.

Amma says, "The sense of ownership is the cause of all tension. If we become an instrument in the hands of God, then we can accomplish all tasks without mental agitation."

Lord Krishna says the same thing in the Bhagavad Gita. He instructs Arjuna: *nimitta mātraṁ bhava*—"Be a mere instrument."[77]

Our burdens of worry and tension dissolve when we remember that we are only an instrument in the hands of the divine. Once, I was asked to deliver a speech during the inaugural session of a conference. My talk went smoothly and although I hadn't been too nervous before I gave it, I felt particularly relaxed once it was over. Finally, I could sit back and enjoy the rest of the conference. Or so I thought. At the end of the second day, the valedictory session was about to start. I was sitting in

[77] Bhagavad Gita 11.33

the audience without a care in the world. Two important guests had arrived to speak for the session. The compére was inviting them to the stage: "I invite Ms. so-and-so, representative of such-and-such an organization, to the stage." And, "I now would like to invite Mr. so-and-so, of such-and-such designation, to the stage." What I heard next caught me completely by surprise: "I invite Brahmacharini Amrita Chaitanya, representative of Mata Amritanandamayi, to the stage." As if on autopilot, I stood up and my legs carried me to the stage where I took my place in the row of dignitaries.

I reassured myself by thinking that maybe I was invited simply to be present on the stage. I recalled that during the inaugural session, a few of the dignitaries seated on the dais hadn't been invited to talk. Surely, they would have told me if I was expected to say something. One of the organizers started the final remarks. Then, turning in my direction he said, "I now invite Brahmacharini Amrita Chaitanya to share a few words."

My heart skipped a beat. Again on autopilot, I stood up and walked to the podium. The organizer whispered to me, "You have five minutes." "Five minutes?" I exclaimed under my breath. "No one told me I'd be asked to talk!"

But there I was, standing at the podium, facing a crowd of people looking at me with expectation. For a split second, I froze. What was I going to say? At that moment, a thought flashed through my mind: "You are only an instrument in the hands of the divine. God will do the talking through you. All you need to do is try your best; the rest is not your responsibility."

With that one thought, I relaxed. I realized I just needed to have the willingness to start and trust that everything would come out alright in the end. Once my mind became calm—with this one powerful, transformative thought—ideas started flowing and I was able to talk confidently. A potentially awkward and embarrassing moment was averted.

Amma says, "We need surrender. Surrender is the confidence that the divine will take care of everything. We can never sleep near the den of a serpent, as we will be in constant fear that the snake will come out and bite us. Anxiety over the future, lack of faith—these are the snakes we carry within. We need to surrender such anxieties at the feet of the divine. We need to put forth our effort and leave the rest to divine will."

If we are able to remember that we are only an instrument, we will be free from fear or anxiety. It is said in the Bhagavatam:

> *yad bāhu-daṇḍābhyudayānujīvino*
> *yadu-pravīrā hyakutobhayā muhuḥ*
>
> The heroes of the Yadu Clan, being protected by the arms of Lord Krishna, always remain fearless in every respect.[78]

We can try to remember that at every moment we are protected by the loving arms of the divine. Then, we will become like a carefree child, knowing all our needs will be taken care of. We will be like our king who relaxed, knowing he was but a trustee and that the responsibility of the kingdom was with his guru. Embracing such an outlook, we will rediscover the beauty and magic we thought were lost with our childhood. Maybe one day I'll get a chance to share this simple stress-remedy with my childhood friend too.

---

[78] Srimad Bhagavatam 1.14.38

Umbrella of Grace

One evening, before bhajans, Amma was talking with a small boy: Amma was sitting on the stage with the musicians and singers, and the child was in front of the stage. He was facing Amma, boldly talking in the mic about all sorts of things. At one point, he announced, "Amma, in the old days, they didn't have umbrellas. So, people would use big leaves instead."

Amma responded as if she was learning something new: "Oh! Is that really so?"

"Yes, Amma, it really is!" came the prompt reply.

Amma then said, "Do you know that there is an umbrella within us? That is the real umbrella, the one that gives us real security and protection. But to open it, we have to press a button. That is the button of our ego."

There is a profound lesson for all of us in these simple words spoken by Amma to a four-year-old. Amma went on to explain that the umbrella within each of us is the umbrella of grace. Our ego tells us that we are in charge of our life, that we know what is good for us and that things should go according to our plan. This sense of "I," this sense of being in-charge, blocks us from receiving God's grace. Humbling our ego and handing over the reins to the divine is what Amma means by saying we have to press the button of our ego to open the umbrella of grace.

Amma says, "God is impartial. He is beyond all differences, has equal vision and is unattached. We should be able to bow our head and surrender, having firm faith in God's will. If we have this, we will certainly receive God's grace. We will be able to maintain peace and contentment in both good and bad times, in gain as well as loss, in success as well as failure."

I'd like to share with you the story of a friend of mine. She was living in the US with her husband and two sons. The family would see Amma every year when she visited the US. One year, Amma told her and her husband that she felt they should move to India. This came as a complete shock to them. They were comfortable in their life in America. Moving the whole family to India was definitely not part of their plans. But their faith in Amma and their surrender to her words made them put their plans and fears aside. They packed up their affluent lives in the US and came to India. They adjusted to living in one simple room in the ashram.

A few years later, their world turned upside down when my friend was diagnosed with breast cancer. It was a rapidly multiplying tumor. The treatment would include surgery and eight rounds of chemotherapy and radiation. Amma advised her to undergo the full treatment as recommended by the doctors.

It wasn't easy. The night after the surgery, she suffered agonizing pain. In those moments of agony, Amma called her on the phone. Amma said four simple sentences: "Don't be sad. It will pass. Be brave. Amma is always with you."

My friend said, "The faith and self-confidence I got from these words carried me through those difficult times. More importantly, they helped me to surrender and accept the situation. My treatment was not easy, but I felt protected and taken care of throughout. I received my full treatment at Amma's hospital with Amma's beautiful smiling photo in every room. The chemotherapy nurses who took care of me were very loving and compassionate."

Throughout the treatment, she felt she was under the protection of the divine. Both my friend and her husband say that they can't imagine the nightmare this episode would have been if they had remained in the US. He would have had to keep working throughout her illness to keep their health insurance going. Being a doctor, that would have been particularly risky considering the conditions with the COVID pandemic. In America, it would have been quite a traumatic, isolated time for their sons. Instead, they were surrounded by support and love from the ashram community.

In their act of moving to the ashram, they had bowed down before the will of the divine. That was the "pressing down" of the button of the ego. That caused the umbrella of grace to open and protect them during those challenging times.

No one can avoid suffering. It is part and parcel of life. At the same time, if we have an attitude of surrender, this makes us open to grace. With that grace, even the toughest of situations becomes manageable.

Amma says, "God's grace is everywhere, at all times. We must surrender our lives to God with an attitude of humility. All of our problems and obstacles will then be reduced to a minimum. It will make us recipients to God's grace."

Surrendering to God doesn't only mean surrendering to a personal form. Amma says God is not separate from creation. As such, God can be described simply as existence or life force. Viewed like this, the "pressing down of the ego button" means developing an attitude of humility towards existence, developing a faith in life. Rather than being rigid in our ideas about how situations should unfold, we can try to develop a trust in the flow of life. We can try to remain flexible and receptive in our efforts, rather than seeking to remain in control; we can keep our mind open to something greater than our individual selves.

Everything is a Gift

It is said that Lord Buddha once asked a disciple, "If a person is struck by an arrow, is it painful?"

The disciple replied, "It is."

Then the Buddha asked, "If the person is struck by a second arrow, is that even more painful?"

The disciple replied again, "It is."

"In life, we cannot always control the first arrow," explained the Buddha. "However, the second arrow is our reaction to the first. And with this second arrow comes the possibility of choice."

The first arrow represents the event or difficulty that causes us stress as well as our immediate feelings regarding it—perhaps sorrow, anger or fear. For instance, we may not be included in a social or professional event and immediately feel hurt, or we may find ourselves stuck in traffic and feel frustrated.

The next arrow comes when we hold on to such negative feelings, leaning into them and allowing them to fester. Whether that second arrow strikes us or not is up to us. Here are some examples of second arrows: "Why do such things always have to happen to me? I always have such bad luck." "What are people going to think about me?" "Was I left out on purpose? Or was it just that no one cared enough to remember to include me?" "I'm never going to be able to do this; it's going to fail, and everyone will know about it." "I'm sure she did it deliberately. I know she has something against me."

Getting caught in such secondary reactions—negative feelings, thoughts and judgments —causes us a lot of suffering.

Losing a job, falling out with someone we are close to, meeting with failure, getting injured—these are all difficult experiences. But we tend to add to our pain through unhelpful thought patterns. And these are usually more painful than the first arrow. We can't control when and if the first arrows strike us. Everyone's life is a mix of pleasure and pain, success and failure, favorable and unfavorable circumstances. The second arrow, however, *is* within our control. Spirituality teaches us how to eliminate the pain we suffer from this second arrow—the additional pain that we inflict upon ourselves, often without even realizing it.

Amma says we should focus on changing the *manasthiti* (inner attitude) rather than the *paristhiti* (external environment). This changing of our attitude is the very purpose of spirituality.

Accepting situations that are beyond our control is necessary for our peace of mind. Sometimes people misinterpret this teaching. They think that spirituality tells us to passively accept everything, even mistreatment or abuse—to remain as victims of whatever life brings. In reality, it is just the opposite. Spirituality does not teach us to be passive and avoid facing challenging situations. Consider what Krishna tells Arjuna in the Bhagavad Gita. He tells him to *fight*. Through that, Krishna encourages us all to let go of our cowardice and engage in action bravely. Amma often reminds us that we are not helpless and dependent, like little kittens. We have tremendous inner strength and therefore should have the courage to roar like lions. We are not candles that need to be lit by someone else; we are the self-luminous sun. So, spirituality is not about being passive.

Still, certain aspects of our life are beyond our control. There are circumstances that we cannot avoid. We may have an inherited health condition, for example. Or there may be difficult people who we have to interact with, at work or at home. Things may not always go the way we wish they would. This is why we should try to develop a level of acceptance. There are situations in which it is important to put forth external efforts towards improving or changing an aspect of our life or of society. Simultaneously, within us, we should try to develop acceptance. This is for our own sake. If we go on resisting a situation, that resistance will bring stress, and turn into bitterness. All we'll gain is extra wrinkles and gray hair. Whereas if at some level we are able to accept the situation, it gives us poise and strength.

Accepting the situation may not seem like an appealing option. But Amma gives us a way to transform that acceptance into something beautiful, something that can enrich our lives: She tells us, "Accept with *prasāda-buddhi*.[79] When we receive prasad from the temple, we don't say, 'This rice pudding is too sweet' or 'The rice is undercooked.' Rather, we accept it with love and reverence." Let us not limit God to the temple. Lord Krishna says in the Bhagavad Gita:

> *sarvataḥ pāṇi-pādaṁ tat sarvato'kṣi-śiro-mukham*
> *sarvataḥ śrutimalloke sarvam āvṛtya tiṣṭhati*

> With hands and feet everywhere, with eyes, heads and mouths everywhere, with ears everywhere, he exists in the world, enveloping all.[80]

If we can perceive that the whole world is pervaded by the divine, everywhere we go becomes God's temple. Everything that comes our way becomes something to be received with reverence and love.

---

[79] With an attitude of reverence, like one receives prasad, or blessed offering, in the temple

[80] Bhagavad Gita 13.14

Amma often says, *Kṣētrattil janikkām kṣētrattil marikkaru-tu*—"We can be born in the temple, but we shouldn't die in one." This means temples can be the beginning, or the initial steps, of our spiritual life, but shouldn't be seen as its goal. They are a means, not the end. God is not limited to any specific place. God is everywhere, unlimited consciousness, infinity.

Once, I felt let down by a person I held in great esteem—someone who was very important to me. I was told that that person had said something untrue about me. When I was told this, I instantly felt very hurt. I felt like crying. I didn't want to cry in public, so I started heading towards my room.

While walking, I suddenly recalled Amma's words, "Pause before you react to any situation." That moment was a moment of contemplation. I started telling myself, "Wait a minute, you know that all situations come from the divine. So, in reality, this incident actually holds an opportunity for you to learn and grow."

With this shift in attitude, the upset feeling disappeared as if by magic. By the time I reached my room and closed the door behind me, the tears that had been on the verge of falling had been re-absorbed. Rather than crying, I found myself beaming. I was filled with gratitude, as I felt that this little incident was a gift from the Universe—in my perspective, a gift from my guru —to teach me not to be too concerned about what others think of me.

It is not possible for us to change our attitude overnight. Rather, it is something that we have to practice patiently, something we have to train ourselves to do. We become good at whatever we practice. If we practice worrying and reacting, we will become experts at worrying and reacting. Whereas if we practice accepting what life brings us, we will become good at that. If we strive to accept small issues as prasad,[81] we will develop the strength to maintain a positive attitude towards bigger challenges that come our way. It's like a muscle that grows stronger. If we do this, we will soon become strong enough to view every situation that comes to us not as something we need to fight or resist, but as something we can learn from.

[81] Consecrated offerings distributed at the end of worship

Optimistic Faith

Amma says, "A person endowed with faith in the supreme holds on to that principle when a crisis occurs. It is this faith that gives us a strong and balanced mind, enabling us to confront any trying situation."

There was a sage called Uttanka. He lived in the Maru Desert. He had been granted a divine blessing by Lord Krishna, which enabled him to summon water at will simply by invoking Krishna's name. The Lord had said, "Uttanka, whenever you remember me, water will be available to you."

On a particularly hot day, Uttanka was walking in the desert. He was exhausted and extremely thirsty. He remembered his blessing and prayed to Krishna. Immediately, a naked, dirty chandala[82] appeared before him. He had a muddy pot in his hand. He was surrounded by filthy dogs. He handed Uttanka the dirty pot. Uttanka reluctantly looked inside. He saw the insect infested water covered with a layer of moss and felt like throwing up.

The man said, "Go on, drink it." Uttanka gave it back saying, "No, just take it back." The man and the dogs then vanished.

Uttanka turned towards Krishna in his mind. He said, "Lord, what is this? Why are you sending me such unpalatable water?" He then heard a divine voice, "O Uttanka, when you were thirsty and remembered me, I requested Indra to offer you amrita, the nectar of immortality, to quench your thirst forever. Indra was unwilling. I finally convinced him. He agreed on the

---

[82] outcaste

condition that he would appear as a chandala. The amrita would be disguised as dirty water. I agreed, assuming you would have absolute faith in me."

Amma says, "Without faith, we are full of fear. Fear cripples the body and mind, paralyzing us, whereas faith opens our hearts and leads us to love."

Uttanka had lacked faith in Krishna. He had been put off by the "packaging" of Krishna's gift. In our life too there will be times when challenges come our way. Such difficult situations may test our faith. We may fail to recognize the divine in them. In such situations, we can try to maintain the faith that there is something positive in whatever life brings us. This way, any difficulty can turn into a blessing. It depends on our attitude, on our faith, on our openness.

The experience of a devotee of Amma who is working as a doctor in New York illustrates this principle. The hospital where she worked was restructured to handle the influx of patients when the COVID pandemic hit. This was the beginning of a challenging time for her. Many of her patients were very sick, and the treatment that might help them was very limited. In her own words, it was an emotionally draining and physically exhausting time.

Soon, she realized that this would be more of a marathon than a sprint. COVID was here to stay, and each day saw more and more patients. It quickly became overwhelming. She was in this continuous cycle of hospital and home. She'd return to her flat exhausted after every 12-hour shift.

One day when she arrived at the hospital, she received some news: She had been reassigned to a different building, half a mile from the main hospital. Hearing this, she felt very annoyed. She was unfamiliar with the new place. It felt like additional stress on top of what was already a stressful situation.

As if that wasn't enough, that day there was an intense thunderstorm. She walked in the rain to her car. She drove to the new parking area and had another walk through the rain to the building. All the while she was complaining and grumbling about the situation to herself.

But the next day, the weather was clear. With the coming of the clear sky, there was also a shift in her attitude. She resolved to approach the situation with an open mind and optimistic faith. She decided to walk from the main hospital to the building. During the 15-minute walk, she chanted the Mrityunjaya mantra[83] for her very sick patients.

In her own words: "It was such a beautiful experience. I got to enjoy the bright morning sun, the flowers along the way, the fresh air. I felt rejuvenated. Chanting the mantra helped to focus my mind and prepare me for seeing my patients. I felt less stressed even though the circumstances remained the same. From then on, I looked forward to my walks every single day. I felt grateful for this beautiful gift."

This woman's optimism and faith enabled her to learn from this situation. She felt thankful for this experience for teaching her how optimistic faith can help to transform even stressful situations into ones of grace. Uttanka had not been able to recognize the Lord's prasad in the disguise of the dirty water. Our doctor's faith enabled her to recognize a special gift, even when it came in the disguise of a challenging situation.

Amma says, "Nothing can harm a true believer. Faith can give us immense strength. All of life's obstacles, whether created by human beings or by nature, will crumble when they come up against our firm and stable faith."

---

[83] A powerful mantra for health, believed to ward off calamities and prevent untimely death

We needn't be discouraged thinking that we lack faith—be it faith in God, or in life, or in ourselves (in reality, these are all the same). Faith isn't something we are necessarily born with, but something we have to nurture. Whether we realize it or not, faith is an integral part of our daily life. When we sit down on a chair, we trust that it will not break under our weight. When we cross the road, we trust we will not be hit by a car. When we enter a room, we trust the ceiling is not going to collapse onto our heads. Without such forms of trust or faith we wouldn't be able to live. So, it's a question of working on this faith of ours, refining it into a tool in our favor. The idea is to expand it so it encompasses every aspect of our day-to-day existence. By nurturing it gradually, extending its reach to permeate our lives, we will learn to genuinely trust in the flow of life; we will develop the inner strength to face whatever challenges come our way with confidence.

Glossary of common Sanskrit words

ahimsa: non-violence

archana: chanting of the 108 or 1,000 names of a particular deity.

ashram: a place where spiritual seekers and aspirants live or visit, in order to lead a spiritual life. It is usually the home of a spiritual master who guides the aspirants.

Bhagavad Gita: 'Song of the Lord,' 700 verses in which Lord Krishna advises Arjuna, as they stand on the battlefield before the Mahabharata War. It contains practical spiritual guidance and sums up the essence of Vedic wisdom.

bhajan: devotional song in praise of the divine.

brahmacharini: celibate female disciple who practices spiritual disciplines under a guru's guidance; brahmachari is the male equivalent.

darshan: audience with a holy person or a vision of the divine. Amma's signature darshan is a hug.

dharma: 'that which upholds.' Generally refers to the harmony of the universe, a virtuous code of conduct, sacred duty or eternal law.

Mahabharata: ancient Indian epic (see summary on page 267).

mahatma: great-soul; someone who has attained spiritual realization.

Malayalam: language spoken in the Indian state of Kerala.

mantra: a sacred syllable, word or phrase repeated for meditation and spiritual upliftment.

prasad: blessed offering or gift from a holy person or temple, often in the form of food.

puja: ritualistic or ceremonial worship.

Ramayana: ancient Indian epic (see summary on page 264).

Sanatana Dharma: 'Eternal Way of Life,' the ancient spiritual wisdom of India.

satsang: spiritual discourse.

Srimad Bhagavatam: also known as Bhagavatam, a Sanskrit composition that narrates the life, pastimes and teachings of various incarnations of Lord Vishnu, chiefly that of Lord Krishna.

Upanishad: portions of the Vedas dealing with Self-knowledge.

Vedas: most ancient of all scriptures. The Vedas were 'revealed' to the seers in their deep meditation.

yajña: ritualistic worship in which oblations are offered into a fire while mantras are chanted; spirit of offering.

A Short Summary of the Ramayana

Dasharatha, the emperor of Ayodhya, had four sons: Rama, Bharata, Lakshmana and Shatrughna. Rama, the eldest, was considered an incarnation of Lord Vishnu and embodied all virtues. He married Sita, the princess of a neighbouring kingdom. In a dramatic turn of events, he was exiled to the forest for 14 years through the plotting of Queen Kaikeyi, his brother Bharata's mother. Sita and Lakshmana (Rama's devoted brother) willingly accompanied him into exile. King Dasharatha died of grief. With a heavy heart, Bharata agreed to rule Ayodhya in Rama's name until his return. In the forest, Sita was abducted by Ravana, the demon king of Lanka. Rama, with the help of the monkey king, Sugriva, and his minister Hanuman, located Sita in Lanka and set off with an army to rescue her. They attacked Lanka, defeated and killed Ravana, and rescued Sita. They returned to Ayodhya, and Rama was crowned king.

Characters from the Ramayana

Bharata: Rama's brother, Dasharatha's second son

Dasharatha: King of Ayodhya, Rama's father. He had three wives—Kausalya, Kaikeyi and Sumitra

Hanuman: Sugriva's helper, a wise monkey who becomes very devoted to Rama

Kausalya: Rama's mother, Dasharatha's main wife

Jatayu: Referred to as "King of the vultures," friend of Dasharatha and well-wisher of Rama

Kaikeyi: Bharata's mother, Dasharatha's favorite wife

Lakshmana: Rama's younger brother

Rama: Hero of the Ramayana, incarnation of the God Vishnu, eldest son of Dasharatha

Ravana: Demon king of Lanka, who abducted Sita

Sita: Beloved wife of Rama

Sugriva: Monkey king who played a crucial role in aiding Rama in his quest to find Sita

Sumitra: Mother of Lakshmana and Shatrughna, Rama's two youngest brothers

Ramayana: A Simple Family Tree

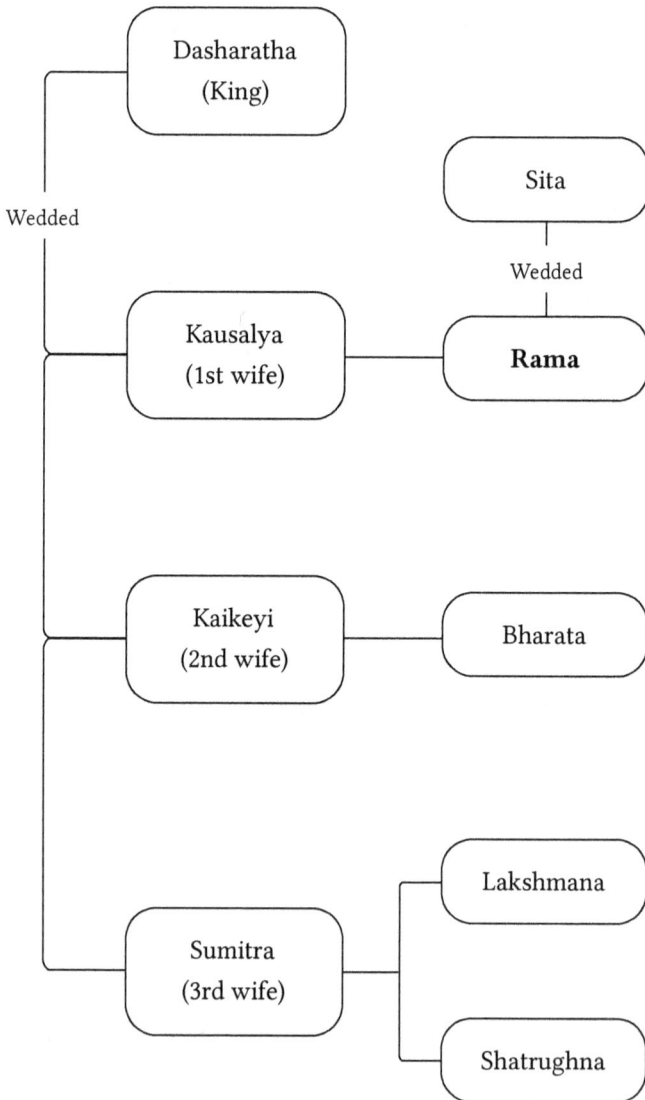

```
                    ┌──────────────┐
                    │  Dasharatha  │
                    │    (King)    │
                    └──────────────┘
                                                    ┌──────────────┐
                                                    │     Sita     │
   Wedded                                           └──────────────┘
                                                         Wedded
                    ┌──────────────┐          ┌──────────────┐
                    │   Kausalya   │──────────│     Rama     │
                    │  (1st wife)  │          └──────────────┘
                    └──────────────┘


                    ┌──────────────┐          ┌──────────────┐
                    │   Kaikeyi    │──────────│   Bharata    │
                    │  (2nd wife)  │          └──────────────┘
                    └──────────────┘

                                               ┌──────────────┐
                                               │  Lakshmana   │
                                               └──────────────┘
                    ┌──────────────┐
                    │   Sumitra    │
                    │  (3rd wife)  │
                    └──────────────┘
                                               ┌──────────────┐
                                               │  Shatrughna  │
                                               └──────────────┘
```

A Short Summary of the Mahabharata

The Kuru kingdom was ruled by Dhritarashtra, who was born blind. Due to his disability, he gave the throne to his younger brother, Pandu. Pandu married Kunti and Madri. He had five virtuous sons known as the Pandavas. Dhritarashtra and his wife, Gandhari, had 100 sons, known as the Kauravas.

Pandu died an untimely death, leaving his sons to the care of his brother Dhritarashtra. But Duryodhana, the eldest of the Kauravas, seized the opportunity to make a bid for the throne. The dispute escalated to a bitter rivalry between the virtuous Pandavas and the unrighteous Kauravas. Duryodhana tried to murder his cousins, but they managed to escape and later returned to ask for their share of the kingdom. In a game of dice, Duryodhana used fraud to beat Yudhishthira, the eldest of the Pandavas, resulting in the Pandavas and their wife Draupadi being exiled for 13 years. Upon their return, Duryodhana refused to give them anything, making war the only option. In the terrible conflict Krishna stood by the Pandavas as their wise adviser. The Bhagavad Gita, the sacred dialogue between Lord Krishna and Arjuna, took place on the battlefield just before the war began. Tragically, most of the main characters lost their life in the war. The Pandavas did win, but their victory came at a very high cost.

Characters from the Mahabharata

Arjuna: Second of the Pandava brothers, skilled archer to whom Krishna instructed the Bhagavad Gita on the battlefield

Bhima: Third of the Pandava brothers

Bhishma: Uncle to both the Pandavas and Kauravas. He had made a vow of celibacy and loyalty to whoever occupied the throne of Hastinapura, which bound him to fight on the side of the unrighteous Kauravas

Dhritarashtra: Blind Kuru king, father of the Kauravas

Draupadi: Beautiful princess who married all five Pandava brothers

Duryodhana: Eldest of the Kauravas

Gandhari: Wife of Dhritarashtra, mother of the 100 Kaurava brothers

Karna: Great archer, close friend of Duryodhana. After the war the Pandavas found out that Karna actually was their brother

Krishna: Kunti's nephew, divine incarnation of Lord Vishnu. He supported the Pandavas during the war

Kunti: Wife of Pandu, mother of the three eldest Pandavas (Yudhishthira, Arjuna, Bhima)

Madri: Second wife of Pandu, mother of the two youngest Pandavas. She took her own life upon the death of her husband

Yudhishthira: Eldest Pandava brother

Mahabharata: A Simple Family Tree

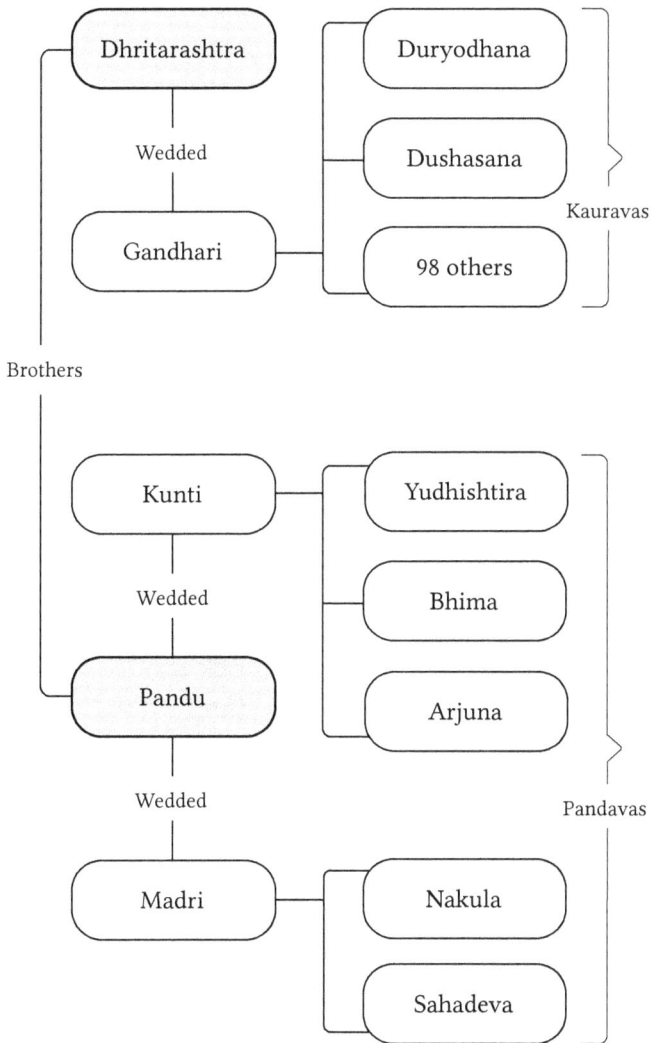

Dhritarashtra		Duryodhana
Wedded		Dushasana
Gandhari		98 others

Kauravas

Brothers

Kunti		Yudhishtira
Wedded		Bhima
Pandu		Arjuna

Pandavas

Wedded		
Madri		Nakula
		Sahadeva

Pronunciation Guide

IAST transliteration scheme has been used for Sanskrit sentences and terms. The following is a pronunciation guide for the same.

Vowels can be short or long:

a – as 'u' in but	ā – as 'a' in far
e – as 'a' in may	ē – as 'a' in name
i – as 'i' in pin	ī – as 'ee' in meet
o – as in oh	ō – as 'o' in mole
u – as 'u' in push	ū – as 'oo' in hoot
	ai - as in sky
	au - as in town

ṛ – as ri in crisp, pronounced with the tip of the tongue bent slightly back towards the roof of the mouth
ḥ – pronounce 'aḥ' like 'aha,' 'iḥ' like 'ihi,' and 'uḥ' like 'uhu.'

Some consonants are aspirated (e.g. kh); others are not (e.g. k). The examples given below are only approximate:

k – as 'k' in 'kite'	kh – as 'ckh' in 'Eckhart'
g – as 'g' in 'give'	gh – as 'g-h' in 'dig-hard'
c – as 'c' in 'cello'	ch – as 'ch-h' in 'staunch-heart'
j – as 'j' in 'joy'	jh – as 'dgeh' in 'hedgehog'
p – as 'p' in 'pine'	ph – as 'ph' in 'up-hill'
b – as 'b' in 'bird'	bh – as 'bh' in 'rub-hard'

r – as 'r' in ride
ñ – as 'ny' in 'canyon' ṅ – as 'ng' in 'sing'

The letters ḍ, ṭ, ṇ are pronounced with the tip of the tongue against the hard palate, the others with the tip against the teeth.
ṭ – as 't' in 'tub'   ṭh – as 'th' in 'lighthouse'

ḍ – as 'd' in 'dove'   ḍh – as 'dh' in 'red-hot'
ṇ – as 'n' in 'naught'
ḷ – as 'l' in 'revelry'
ś – as 'sh' in 'shine'
ṣ – pronounced like ś, except the tip of the tongue is bent slightly back towards the roof of the mouth

With double consonants the sound is pronounced twice:
cc – as 'tc' in 'hot chip'
jj – as 'dj' in 'red jet'

The letters ṫ and ṙ (in Malayalam) are pronounced with the tip of the tongue touching the roof of the mouth just behind the teeth.

Acknowledgements

I would like to start by expressing my heartfelt gratitude to Swamiji—Swami Amritaswarupananda Puri—for his steadfast support and for providing the opportunity for delivering these talks. Special thanks also to Rajani Chechi for her suggestions and invaluable assistance with the Malayalam phase.

I feel very fortunate for the dedicated help of those who contributed significantly to the realization of this book: my mum Sue, Brahmachari Satvamrita Chaitanya, Brahmachari Sachinmayamrita Chaitanya, Karnaki, Veena, and Kripa. Countless others helped me with their suggestions, encouragement, feedback and ideas—Ambujam deserves a special mention here. A special thanks also to Mukti for her beautiful artwork and design skills for the cover, as well as Jagannath for the layout of the book.

Amma often likens the ashram to a rock tumbler, where numerous stones with rough edges are gathered and tumbled together. In this process, they rub against each other, smoothing out their sharp edges, transforming into lustrous stones. With this in mind, I also have to express my gratitude to all my fellow stones in the tumbler. For it is interactions with them that have provided many of the stories in this book: situations which made me learn about the unhelpful emotions and foolish workings of my mind!